GATHERED STONES

Divine Encounters in Everyday Life

Michael L. Lyle

• Canada • UK • Ireland • USA •

Note for Librarians: a cataloguing record for this book that includes Dewey Decimal
Classification and US Library of Congress numbers is available from the Library and
Archives of Canada. The complete cataloguing record can be obtained from their online
database at:
www.collectionscanada.ca/amicus/index-e.html
ISBN 1-4120-5726-4
Printed in Victoria, BC, Canada

*Printed on paper with minimum 30% recycled fibre. Trafford's print shop runs on "green energy" from
solar, wind and other environmentally-friendly power sources.*

Offices in Canada, USA, Ireland and UK
This book was published *on-demand* in cooperation with Trafford Publishing.
On-demand publishing is a unique process and service of making a book available for
retail sale to the public taking advantage of on-demand manufacturing and Internet
marketing. On-demand publishing includes promotions, retail sales, manufacturing,
order fulfilment, accounting and collecting royalties on behalf of the author.

Book sales for North America and international:
Trafford Publishing, 6E–2333 Government St.,
Victoria, BC V8T 4P4 CANADA
phone 250 383 6864 (toll-free 1 888 232 4444)
fax 250 383 6804; email to orders@trafford.com
Book sales in Europe:
Trafford Publishing (UK) Ltd., Enterprise House, Wistaston Road Business Centre,
Wistaston Road, Crewe, Cheshire CW2 7RP UNITED KINGDOM
phone 01270 251 396 (local rate 0845 230 9601)
facsimile 01270 254 983; orders.uk@trafford.com
Order online at:
trafford.com/05-0624

10 9 8 7 6 5 4 3

For everything there is a season, and a time for every matter under heaven . . . a time to throw away stones, and a time to gather stones together . . .

Ecclesiastes 3:1&5a, NRSV

Here I raise mine Ebenezer;
hither by thy help I'm come;
and I hope, by thy good pleasure,
safely to arrive at home.

Robert Robinson, from the hymn
Come, Thou Fount of Every Blessing

To each the boulders that have fallen to each.
And some are loaves and some so nearly balls
We have to use a spell to make them balance:
"Stay where you are until our backs are turned!"
We wear our fingers rough with handling them.

Robert Frost, from *Mending Wall*

For Brenda

Table of Contents

Foreword

Two years ago my son posted over his desk a motto that read: "Lord, just show me the way and I'll do all the work." I call this "Martin's Prayer." Martin is Mexican, he was baptized in the Catholic Church, and so far as I can tell has never made confession, taken communion, or, except for serving as godparent in the baptism of several of his nieces and nephew, has not participated in any of the rituals of the Church except on the day of La Virgin de Guadalupe, December 12, when he takes flowers, lights a candle, and prays at the shrine of the Virgin. A large framed picture of The Virgin of Guadalupe hangs over his bed.

In his thirty years, Martin has encountered more problems and obstacles than most of us can even imagine. His favorite metaphor is the wall without a door. Some-times, he says, the walls surround him—even retreat isn't possible. Several months ago, he felt, not just that the walls were all there, but that they were closing in on him. For the first time ever, I heard him express doubt that God was really showing him the way. He was willing to do the work, but where was the way. Then after a week of despair and feeling abandoned, a door opened. How had he gotten through that week? By telling himself, and me, over and over the stories of all the difficulties he had faced and gotten through. God had not forsaken him, simply challenged him. He had, to use the metaphoric title of Mike Lyle's book, "gathered stones."

It is a truism (I wish I could claim to have invented it) that the stories we tell represent the values we embrace and live by. Whether it is the classical myths, the stories from the Bible, the parables of Jesus, Dante's Divine Comedy, the stories we collectively tell from our family's memory, the novels of Charles Dickens, the poems of William Butler Yeats, the short stories of Flannery O'Connor: all represent at some time and for some people their highest values. With words and stories we don't just describe the world; we *create,* we *invent* the world. With our words we assign meaning, we approve or we denigrate, we accept or we reject, we laud or we condemn.

With our words we make our stories, we write our creeds, we outline our doctrines, we declare our principles; and then we engage in debate about what our words really mean: "all men are created equal," "equal justice under the law," "saved by faith alone," "faith without works is dead," "God will provide," "the will of God," and a hundred etceteras.

When I moved to the Great Southwest thirteen years ago, I began the cultural initiation which involves learning to eat chili. At first, probably like every novice, I always asked "Which is hotter, the red or the green?" And I would choose the least hot. I learned eventually as everyone must that red and green taste different, and finally that hotter is better. I now have a new test: if I eat chili and the top of my head begins to tingle and I get sweaty around the eyes, then the chili is good. The "chili effect" has become my litmus for good writing. Melville's *Moby-Dick* is always my prime example. There are passages there that always induce the chili effect, no matter how many times I have read them.

I have known Mike Lyle for more years than I remember, but from whatever year he was a college freshman—maybe thirty-five years. While we have not visited together in probably over twenty years now, we have always stayed in some communication, with sometimes lapses of several years. For the past several years, we have had a continuous and sometimes intense email correspondence that has frequently engaged questions of faith, belief, institutional religion, the historical Jesus, etc. I have frequently told Mike that if I were a member of his congregation, hearing his sermons weekly, I would no doubt be a better person. For several years, I have received his weekly church bulletin, for which Mike usually writes a commentary entitled "Beside Still Waters." No matter what mail has come that day, I always read his BSW first.

Therefore, when Mike asked me to write a Foreword to the collection of stories he calls "Gathered Stones," I immediately accepted without any consideration of what credentials I had for doing so. In matters of theology I am naïve, I am in matters of faith and religion a skeptic or an agnostic, I am not a member of any church and have not attended any religious service except for weddings and funerals for almost twenty years.

What moves me in Mike's writing, however, is a sense of his constant care for the basic human need for love, for compassion, for understanding, for relief. These stories relate experiences from his ministry that explore his own quests for translating the gospel he loves into the real experiences of people's lives. He is not afraid to admit his mistakes, to learn from his failures. He translates his faith into deeds. These are human stories. They are stories that embrace those values that we might live by.

I began by writing about "Martin's Prayer": "Lord, just show me the way and I'll do all the work." If my initial response to that prayer was that it was naïve and simplistic, Mike Lyle's writing has helped me to understand both the profound spirituality and the translation of belief into action which it states. And the simpler the statement of creed, the better our chances of translating it into life.

LaMarr Smith
El Paso, Texas
February 2005

Introduction

E*benezer* is from the Hebrew, meaning *stone of help*. I have needed many, as do we all.

On a bitterly cold November night decades ago, my father was critically injured in an automobile accident. He was on his way back to the Army base where he was stationed awaiting deployment to the Korean Conflict. He was a pharmacist with a hospital unit and had just spent Thanksgiving with his family. My mother was six months pregnant with me and all three of us lost our anticipated future that night. My parents were prepared for the pain of a long separation, but not for what befell.

The remainder of our three lives became response to this tragic accident that robbed my father of himself (his education, the knowledge of how to do even the simplest things, any memory of his former life) and us of him. After waking from three months in a coma, he had to be re-introduced to his family as if a stranger. The person he was had been lost. My mother remained faithfully with him, dedicated to his care, until her death 53 years later.

I've spent my life looking for my father. I've searched old photographs and every comment made by those who knew him "before," hoping for some additional clue. I've listened to every breeze, sifted every silence, wondering if he might be there.

When I'm with my father, sometimes a word, a gesture, or a smile will startle me with the feeling that his true self has shone through, if only for a moment. Sometimes, I even think I recognize him in a word or behavior of my own.

Somewhere along the way, I realized that I was searching for God. The search for the one had become inextricably bound with the search for the other. Whatever the reality, I have a wonderful father.

Throughout my search I've looked for help and have always found it, because God is wonderfully and inexhaustibly good. I've come to think of those people and situations that have helped me make sense of life, and sometimes simply enabled me to survive, as stones of help.

These are some of the insights, some of the remarkable people, some of the stones of help I've discovered and kept along the way. By binding them in this small volume, I hope I've begun to raise my own Ebenezer, just like the old hymn says. I hope my gathered stones will help you identify and gather your own. That is my prayer for you.

Mike Lyle
Roanoke, Virginia
March 2005

Chapter One:

IN THE MIDST OF LIFE

Shootin' the Boot

Before the current emergency address system came along, country folks didn't live at 3019 Dark Hollow Lane. They lived "up Dark Hollow past the old Martin place," and you got there by passing "the ole house where Sam Gordon's mother used to live" and turning in "by the big rock just this side of the bridge."

This particular country parish is bisected by a two-mile stretch of straight-running, two-lane state route. The Methodist church marks the southern end and a country store the northern. From the turkey buzzard's point of view Route 716 must look like a fat, black millipede with lines down its back, most of its legs pulled off and those remaining grown long and twisty. Each remaining leg has grown up against one of the two mountain ridges that form the narrow valley.

I only made it to the very end of one of those twisty legs when I visited the Carpers. It was easier going all the way to the end of the road. No need to look for particular rocks, or abandoned sheds, or dirt turnoffs. Just get started on the right leg of the millipede and drive 'till the road ends.

Motoring down that lane meant leaving the rest of the world behind and like most transitional experiences always left me feeling mixed. The dirt and gravel lane wound between hedgerows, fences and fields of corn. Here and there, small gaps signaled paths and byways leading to individual farms and homesteads. From these, footpaths lit out for places barely imaginable, hidden by evergreens, tucked into hollows, or on the lee side of some enormous, decaying barn.

It was startling for me to realize how many people lived out there, invisible and unmolested by any but their own kin and an occasional neighbor. It was peaceful, but eerily so.

By the time a car rolls up to the Carper place the motorist has slowed down in every kind of way. It's possible to speed along the lane to their house, as the Carper boys frequently demonstrated in huge, rolling clouds of dust, but it's ill advised.

My car first arrived there late one afternoon in high summer. The house, almost surrounded by woods, sat beneath the shade of several large trees. Just to the left of the house, past a couple of small sheds and a huge stack of firewood, a mown field lay baking in the July sun. The house had apparently started small and evolved into what stood before me. It was a house that had been so perfect for two that it had started sprouting bedrooms. It was now a three-son house where the cars parked within feet of the front door.

At this early stage in my career, I hadn't yet sorted out if preachers should phone ahead. I arrived unannounced.

Mr. & Mrs. Carper both worked outside the small community. She was in real estate and he an electrician. The oldest boy was 18, the youngest 12, and the other somewhere in between. The youngest answered my knock at the door. He seemed wary and surprised at first, and then excited. He had been at worship my first Sunday and recognized me. *Hey Todd,* he called back into the dark coolness of the house. *It's the preacher. Get your butt out here.* And then to me, *Hey, Mr. Lyle, come on in.*

I was flattered to be remembered and delighted to receive such a spontaneous and jovial welcome. Todd appeared within seconds and there stood the three of us in the Carper living room/den/dining room. Todd and Andy invited me to sit and so we settled into the worn but comfortable chairs and sofas for a visit.

We made awkward small talk until they tired of it (two minutes tops) and invited me to see their rooms. Each boy in turn took me to his bedroom where I commented on the various posters, sports equipment and eclectic artifacts boys collect. We had about concluded the tour when Andy winked at Todd and suggested he show me what was under the bed.

Todd's mattress sat in a wooden frame atop a low pedestal. The top of the bed didn't look hinged, but it was. Todd lifted it to reveal a small arsenal. There were hunting rifles, shotguns and handguns, as well as automatic and semi-automatic military surplus type weapons. There was even a muzzleloader.

The boys clearly enjoyed the look of amazement on my face as I gawked at their armory. I think I said something clever like, *Wow.* Initially I tried to imagine the Armageddon for which they were preparing. Then I relaxed and realized (hoped) they were simply collectors. Close inspection led me to wonder if even half of their collection was functional, although one never knows about guns.

I commented on the muzzleloader and they assured me it worked. I realized, in the millisecond following my question, that we were going to take it outside. *Ever shot a muzzle loader, Mr. Lyle*? Andy asked with mock innocence. We all knew that we all knew that I hadn't. We all knew that we all knew that I was about to.

By now I had begun feeling like the victim of a conspiracy. It felt like the boys had done this before. What time was it getting to be? Would the elder Carpers be home soon? Would anyone be along ever? Was I with the lost boys?

The boys quickly and efficiently gathered powder and shot. We walked past the sheds and the firewood into the bright field where they asked me to pick a target. I noticed an old boot lying in the field about thirty yards away. *I'll try for that boot*, I said.

The boys loaded the gun, cocked it, and placed it in my hands. They were immensely pleased with everything. Too pleased, I feared.

Having never shot a muzzle loader, not really knowing the Carper boys, and having recently read a newspaper report of a man who had been blinded and hopelessly disfigured when a muzzle loader exploded in his face, I took the gun as a condemned man takes the tray bearing his last meal, with a sense of genuine anticipation pretty much overwhelmed by dread. It didn't help my uneasiness that after I was handed the gun both boys took a step or two backwards. It was as if they too suspected something explosive.

So as they withdrew, I pulled the source of the explosion right up under my nose and looked down the long barrel at the boot. The only thing for certain was that I was going to fire that gun. The future of Christendom would have been secure either way, but my credibility with all the youth, and not a few of the adults, of my new parish rested with my firing that gun.

The only question now was whether or not I would hit the boot. I had discharged a few weapons at a variety of targets over the years. I thought I could hit the boot, if I kept my eyes open, but that was the problem. I knew there was going to be an explosion. I knew I wanted to see my wife and children again, and sunsets, and perhaps even the faces of my grandchildren someday. I knew I was going to close my eyes.

I sighted the boot, took a deep breath, and began to slowly squeeze the trigger. Just as I began squeezing I shut my eyes, tight. The explosion happened as it had for hundreds of years. The ball sped toward its target. I missed the boot by about a foot, kicking up some dust behind it.

Not bad for your first time. Andy said. *Yeah,* said Todd, *lots of people shut their eyes when they fire that thing.* At first I was flattered that Todd might be suggesting that I would have hit the boot if I had kept my eyes open. Then I realized that he was really saying, *Well, at least you fired it.*

I don't think I fully passed muster that afternoon with the Carper boys. They came to church off and on. They were always friendly and polite, but I never felt like they really let me into their world.

I've never been sure how I feel about that either. Might I have eventually raced up and down the lane stirring up great clouds of dust and tempting fate at every turn? Would I have ever hit the boot, seeing the explosion right under my nose? Would I have liked it? Would I have loved it?

I sure loved the supper they served me a while later. I talked with the boys until their mother and older brother came roaring down the lane, each in their own dust-covered vehicle. Mrs. Carper said we needn't wait for Mr. as she laid out, in a remarkably few minutes, fried chicken, corn on the cob, mashed potatoes, green beans, cole slaw, squash and hot rolls. When we pulled our assortment of chairs up to that table covered with steaming food, they didn't ask me to pray, as I would be asked on so many future occasions. Mrs. Carper called upon Todd, seemingly at random, and he prayed effortlessly, naturally, sincerely, over that wonderful food served with such humble grace in that funny little house at the end of the lane.

Is God Home?

Children, in their understandable need to associate abstract concepts with concrete reality, have been known to occasionally associate their pastor with God or Jesus. I simply encountered an unusually virulent strain.

He was the grandson of faithful worshippers whose evangelism of their own family had brought their divorced daughter and her three-year-old son to church. Everyone, of course, was delighted.

After several months of regular attendance, I noticed that the little fellow was greeting me as God; not *Mr. God*, not *the Rev. God*, just *God*. He would shake my hand enthusiastically as I greeted folks at the church door after worship. *Hey God. Goodbye God. How's it goin' God?*

I smiled and answered him. Everyone smiled. It was sooooo cute.

It was cute until it reached that mystical, impossible-to-pinpoint moment when it simply stopped being cute. The other church folk were getting a bit uneasy with my being referred to as God by anyone, regardless of age. My wife and children were beginning to use the term derisively. *Now is that really something that God should be doing?* Or *I'm really surprised to hear God say such a thing.* Stuff like that.

And then the grandparents of the little guy confided in me one Sunday that it was becoming a problem at home. The little tike wouldn't listen to reason. Each family member had tried explaining one on one. All had tried explaining *en mass.* Nothing fazed him.

A few Sundays later his mother tearfully asked me to speak to her son. *It's really starting to get serious now.* "Are we going to see God today?" *he'll ask.* "What does God eat for breakfast?" "Let's go ask God, he'll know what to do." *I'm at the end of my rope. He just won't listen. Could you maybe talk to him? He will listen to you.*

I was being asked to explain to a small child who genuinely believed that I was God (and who was also, I suspect, thinking that God just might make a good surrogate father), that it was all a lie. Try to imagine God explaining to you that God is not God. The potential for long-term theological and psychological devastation was enormous. I had only been a seminary student for a year and a half, but I already knew that they don't cover this kind of stuff there. It's not covered anywhere.

And so after I had greeted the last exiting parishioner (taking as long as possible with each), I looked at the family waiting for me under the shade of the big tree in the churchyard. They weren't budging until I resolved this God thing once and for all. I told them I'd be right there. I decided that my de-divination would go more smoothly if I wasn't wearing my alb, so I ducked into the empty church to disrobe, to compose myself, and to pray. Nothing helped.

So I put on my best version of a confident, benevolent, competent clergy smile and joined the family under the tree. I don't recall what I said, only that it was rambling, embarrassing and completely ineffective. The little guy listened attentively. When I was finished he said, *OK, Bye God.* and headed for the car, leaving me to withstand the withering stares of his frustrated family. It was one of those Sundays when I just skipped lunch altogether.

I don't know if his mother had a brain storm, or if God (having had enough by then as well) gave her a vision, or if the little guy just took one of his notions to chat with God, but things finally came to a head one Sunday morning a few weeks later. I wasn't having a good morning. I'd stayed up too late the night before reworking a sermon that I never did come to like. I'd overslept. My wife was busy with our two daughters and with getting herself ready for the rigors of the morning. I'd had my shower and was standing in our disheveled bedroom in my underwear clipping my fingernails.

A knock came at the back door. *Is God home?* I heard his little voice asking my wife. *Sure honey, he's right back there. Just go right in. Mike, there's somebody here to see you.* She called from the kitchen, with that wicked lilt to her voice that lets me know I'm in for something.

A second later there he stood. The little guy stood in the door of our bedroom staring at me. No, *Hey God.* No, *Mornin' God.* Just staring.

He looked me up and down, slowly, carefully, as I stood there in my underwear clipping my nails. He looked around the messy bedroom. He looked back at me. He bolted. The kitchen door slamming behind him signaled the end of my divinity.

I don't know what he related to his family. He and his mother stopped attending worship. His grandparents kept coming, but we never spoke of the matter again.

The Beatles sing about how *something in the way she moves* makes all the difference. *Everything* about the way I was at that crucial moment assured my young adherent that I was not God. As is often the case when a veil is drawn back, nothing can really be the same again. My descent had been far less dramatic, but just as final as Icarus falling from the sky.

That's Not
What You're Supposed to be Doing

I once heard a bishop say, when addressing an incoming class of ordinands at an Annual Conference session, that, among other things, they would never go to bed again for the rest of their lives not knowing that there was one more visit, one more call, one more act of ministry that they could have accomplished. He was talking about guilt. The bishop was referring to a disease that infects all clergy. It makes us believe that we are subject to a different set of criteria than other Christians. It makes us believe that we are supposed to be holier, more diligent, more self-emptying than everybody else. And so we feel like crap even when we have done our work sacrificially and well.

It's this hopelessly wrong understanding of ministry that causes the breakup of parsonage marriages. It causes depression, alcoholism, suicide, abuse and all sorts of other horrors. It causes clergy to take themselves, their families, others, and life in general far too seriously. It's all bad.

[1 1]

Those who are diligent, dedicated, professional purveyors of ministry will be that regardless. Those who aren't, well, aren't. Guilt hurts us all, and reduces whatever effectiveness we might otherwise have.

Clergy guilt is a devastating virus that erases what God tries to write on our hearts. It makes us tentative and keeps us from courageous creativity that could change the church and change lives. It keeps us from truly loving God and others. The author of the virus designed it that way.

I was most disturbed to hear that bishop make that statement to those fresh, new members of my Conference. I was frustrated, because he was only half right. He was right in mentioning the virus and calling our attention to it. He was wrong in that he perpetuated the virus by implying that it was the way things have to be.

There are those in the church who <u>like</u> to set clergy apart and there are clergy who like <u>being</u> set apart. These people contribute to the ruination of the community that God is constantly working to create among and through us. These people thwart the sense of humanity and wholeness that God works constantly to create within us.

The virus manifests itself in so many ways, and with such surgical skill, that it cannot be too diligently defended against. If the pastor is not at every meeting, every function, every bedside, every crisis, every soccer game, every wedding, every Vacation Bible School, every phone (no one wants an answering machine), every picnic, then someone takes note and makes certain that the note gets posted. If the pastor is present at all of the above she or he will not acquit her or himself perfectly. This too will be taken note of and the note will, in one of the myriad ways that people post notes to one another, get posted. All of this, and still the parsonage yard must appear immaculate, the parsonage children perfect, and the parsonage marriage exemplary. The virus makes so many sick, in so many ways.

One autumn evening when my perfect family and I were enjoying a perfectly appropriate television program, in our perfectly kept parlor/den in our perfectly appointed and maintained double-wide parsonage, with a couple of logs crackling in the Franklin stove that was vented through the roof, we noticed a sizzling sound. It was rain running down the hot stovepipe and dripping onto the top of the hot stove.

As a young pastor who wanted desperately to be perfect, my relaxation with my family was over. Whom should I notify? Or should I fix it myself? What had previous pastors done under similar circumstances? What was expected of me? What was the right thing to do?

The longer I live with my image of Jesus of Nazareth, the more I have come to think that Jesus would have simply left the next morning with his entourage. Among his parting comments to his host would have been straightforward notification that the roof was leaking and in need of repair. So much for WWJD.

But I wasn't Jesus, and since it was a Friday night and the rain was supposed to abate by morning, I decided to wait until Sunday morning and perhaps ask some of the kinder, gentler members of my flock for advice. The first person to whom I turned was Walt.

Walt was one of the pillars of the church. That means he gave large portions of his money, time, and energy to the running of the place. It also meant, in Walt's particular case, that he was a man of great faith who, for that very reason, enjoyed the respect of most of the other members of the church. Walt worked a full-time job in the city and worked around his home and yard in his spare time. Every year he took a trip out west to hunt antelope and elk. Walt was small and wiry with a seemingly unending supply of energy. He used this energy to help others. I felt that Walt approved of me and liked me. I knew that he would let me know, in some loving fashion or other, how I should proceed. I got more than I bargained for.

When I explained my leak to Walt, he simply said, *Don't worry about it. I'll take care of it.* End of conversation. He said every word just right. No condescension or disgust. No probing questions. No looks or innuendoes of any kind. *Don't worry about it. I'll take care of it.*

The following afternoon, Monday, was cold and very windy. We had already changed back to Eastern Standard Time and so it was about dark when I heard Walt's ladder clang up against the gutter outside the parsonage. My family and I were just sitting down to dinner.

If you're a homeowner who is paying a contractor good money to make repairs on your home, you acknowledge that she or he is there and you sit down and enjoy your dinner, or whatever else it is that you might be doing. If you're a pastor, and one of your flock is sacrificially repairing the house you live in, under adverse conditions, after working hard all day at his job, you get up from your warm food and you go out there and you offer your assistance. Usually the pastor stays with the church member the whole time, and helps, and yet STILL FEELS GUILTY. The pastor also feels stupid and confused and very conflicted. Did the pastor not leave his family at the dinner table? Did the pastor not show his family by his actions that someone and something else was more important? Did the pastor not deny her or himself, again?

But that wasn't the case this night. Walt was climbing onto the roof when I got there. *You get right back in that house,* he said.

I began stammering and sputtering about the weather and the hour and how I might be of assistance when he said again, and emphatically, *You get right back in that house and have supper with your family. I'll take care of this. I won't be long.*

And then it just came out of my mouth. I was new enough to the ministry, and young enough, and unguarded enough to just blurt out my true feelings. *But Walt,* I said, *it just doesn't feel right for me to be in there when you're out here repairing my house. I feel like I should be taking care of this myself anyway. I'm really sorry.*

Walt realized, as good teachers always do, that this was a teachable moment. He backed all the way down his ladder and stood on the ground facing me. I can still see his weary, earnest face looking right at mine in that uncomfortable gloom. I can still see the light that shone in those eyes that could fell an elk a mile away.

This is your home Mike, and it should be a safe and comfortable one, but it's not your house. It's the church's house and it's our job to take care of it. You have been called to other work. Fixing leaks on the roof, that's not what you're supposed to be doing. You go in there and eat supper with your family. I'll take care of this. Just do what God has called you to do and don't worry about the rest. It was a message that engraved itself upon my soul as the words were spoken. It was a message delivered with firmness and much love. It was a graceful and important message I would hear again from other voices, in other times and places when I needed it most.

I went inside and ate supper with my family. Walt was on the roof for about ten minutes, and then he went home. God always calls us to the work that is the greatest blessing to us and to others, at least that has proved true for Walt, and for me.

Talismans of Love

Gene was short, but powerfully built and stepped out of his truck looking tired and grouchy. Because I was parked in the middle of his driveway, he had squeezed his truck around my vehicle in order to get into his garage. I was standing beside my car in my swimming trunks laughing and joking with his wife. I'd spent the day lounging around his swimming pool, eating his food, and enjoying the company of his family. He had just arrived home from his grueling daily commute to the city where he worked for the power company.

What a horrible first impression, I thought. Here he is arriving home from a hard day's work to discover that his new minister hasn't been visiting the sick, or even the healthy of the parish, but has rather spent the day lounging by his pool. Because I was so ill at ease, I didn't give him a chance to say anything. I introduced myself and began gushing about how nice his family had been to have me over for a swim on such a hot day. *I know who you are*, he said. *I'm sorry we haven't met until now. I'm glad you're here. Make yourself at home.* He talked with me in such a friendly manner that my concern soon evaporated.

I asked about his work, but it soon became obvious that what he really wanted to talk about was his farm. It wasn't a farm in the sense of chickens and geese scurrying in and out of the barn, goats trotting by with their bells clanging and Lassie at the screen door. It was a farm in the sense of his brick ranch sitting in the middle of 15 acres that backed up against a low mountain ridge. It was a farm in the sense that he owned several head of cattle. It was a farm in the sense that he had a barn in his mind that he wanted to build. It was a farm in his heart.

He showed me where the barn would someday sit. He showed me where the new fence he had in mind would go. He talked about the many projects and improvements that would occur as soon as he found the time and energy. As he talked, the stress of the day's work and the weariness of the long commute fell away. He was home. I watched the power of place working in his soul and spreading across his face.

I'm glad somebody's using the pool, he said. *Makes it worth keeping up when people enjoy it.* We talked for thirty minutes or so. He invited me to stay for supper.

He and his family became our surrogate family. Having left doting parents and grandparents behind when we moved to this, our first pastorate, we must have looked as forlorn and displaced as we were. Gene's family adopted us. We ate Sunday dinner with them every week and lots of meals in between. They were friends, parents, brothers, sisters, confidants, and advisors. They were a Godsend.

During the next 18 months, I watched him return home many times. I saw the effects of his day upon him as he arthe center aisle to the back of the church to "administer" the benediction, I lost it.

The congregation had begun moving. It was like a carefully choreographed dance that had been rehearsed to such perfection that every movement was filled with meaning and executed with breathtaking precision. I still don't know if they had planned it, or ever done it before, or if it was totally spontaneous, but they began moving. They moved out of the pews and into the aisles joining hands as they went. No one said a word. They just moved until we formed a circle around that little worship space. Then the two on either side of me took my trembling hands in theirs and somebody (Walt, I think) said, *OK, now you can give the benediction.*

Except I couldn't. I tried a couple of times, but the words wouldn't come. I just wept. I just stood there in that community of faith and wept at the unutterable grace of the experience and at the searing pain of separation. Finally I said, or rather sputtered, *Thank you.* Then, as I usually do when I can no longer bear the power of the moment, I said something funny and we all laughed and the spell was broken and I began talking with them as they left the church for the little stone building across the parking lot where we would have our last meal together.

The day would find completion later that evening, however, when we had supper with Gene and his family. After dinner, Gene asked our daughters if they would like to go down to the barn. They were happy to oblige. It was on the way home in the car that they shared with us what Gene had given them.

Each girl got a quarter. Each girl got a quarter and a

handwritten note that said no matter how old they got, no matter where in the world they were, no matter what kind of trouble they might be in, no matter what time of day or night, no matter what, to know by that quarter that they could call "Uncle Gene" and that he would come for them, or help them in whatever way they required.

Those coins mean as much to our daughters as any gift they have ever received. They are adults now. The shiny little pocket books of childhood have long since given way to purses of all kinds, but they still have their quarters. The quarters are always with them - talismans of love reminding them of eternal connections that will not let us go.

Anniversary

Arthur and Miriam sit close on the steps of a church half a day's drive from home, their fingers, hands and arms intertwined and their heads leaning together, touching, wondering how something so right could be so messed up.

It's a beautiful, soft evening in early June, 1961. JFK has only been in office 6 months, but his inauguration's promise lingers. Gary Player won the Green Jacket at Augusta National in April and it still feels like the whole world should be pink and green so luscious and hopeful a spring it is. Youthful and optimistic as they are, however, Miriam and Arthur are troubled, because things haven't gone as planned. If they listened to *Moon River* or *Where the Boys Are* on the car radio as they drove expectantly into town, those carefree moments are forgotten.

Arthur and Miriam met and fell in love in the third grade and spent the rest of their lives to this moment frequently together but living apart. Having agreed they could bear it no longer, they chose this church and set this day for their wedding.

They sat together on the church steps for almost an hour in the late afternoon sun. For a while, cars passing back and forth on the busy street in front of the church kept up a reassuring drone of activity as people made their way out of town for the weekend, but after a while it began to grow quiet. They glanced often at Arthur's Timex, but the passing minutes brought them no closer to a solution.

They were due at their honeymoon in a few hours. It wasn't an elaborate trip, even by the standards of 1961, but it was paid for and they were looking forward to it more than anything, so charged were they with anticipation, longing and love.

But they were not married.

Miriam had selected this particular church more than a year before when she came to Winchester with her parents and younger twin brothers for the Apple Blossom Parade. The church had just seemed so beautiful and stately, so perfect for her and Arthur's special day.

It had never occurred to anyone that there might be complications at the church. Miriam couldn't imagine anything but happiness, kindness and grace occurring at a church like this.

Thanks to Miriam's good memory and solid sense of direction, they had driven straight to it. They even found the kindly pastor still in his study, working on Sunday's sermon just like Miriam had imagined. He talked with them and assured them he would be happy to officiate their wedding, but that they needed a license. He told them to hurry down to the courthouse, because the offices would soon be closing. If they were too late, he said they could telephone him at home to make arrangements for the following week.

They hurried, but finding their away around an unfamiliar city proved time consuming. The courthouse was locked up tight for the weekend by the time they finally found it and the church was locked up too by the time they got back.

They had no license, the preacher's phone number, each other, a paid-for honeymoon, and a determination not to do anything stupid. They were eager to prove themselves more than the "just kids" that most folks *treated* them like, and *talked* to them like, and talked *about* them like. They weren't about to call home.

They agreed that these weren't the right conditions under which to make such important decisions, so they decided not to try and resolve everything right then and there and to take things one step at a time. The only thing they knew for certain was that they were going on that honeymoon.

The honeymoon was everything they had imagined and more and provided a better place from which to make plans. They still didn't know what to do, but they knew they couldn't lie to their families and friends and they WERE expected home. Even though they weren't sure what they would say, or how they would say it, they were sure they didn't want to cause needless worry, and so they headed for home, believing that the right words would come when they needed them.

They arrived on schedule to find their families and friends waiting with a surprise reception party in their honor. It was all so beautiful and perfect. Everybody was so happy. Nobody asked them much of anything, simply assuming that everything had gone fine.

To their parents, brothers and sisters, grandparents, aunts and uncles, cousins, neighbors, friends and community they were married. And the more everybody *acted* like they were married the more it came to *feel* like they were married. Before long they *were* married, except they *weren't*.

They kept meaning to take care of that important, missing technicality, but it became more and more difficult as time passed. Their welcome-home reception gave way to jobs, church work, two daughters and a son, and eventually the promise of grandchildren. As the years passed and life kept happening all around them, it became less and less important that the courthouse had been closed back there in June of '61. Sometimes they talked of slipping away for a weekend and "making it legal," but they never got around to it.

They never got around to it, because there was something else. They didn't talk about it much in the early years, but as time passed it increasingly arose as a topic between them. They kept remembering. They kept returning to that June afternoon on the church steps, their wedding day.

They remembered the decisions they had made, and not made. They remembered what they had wanted from that day, what they had gotten from that day, and how the decisions of that day had affected their lives. They never thought they had lived a lie. In fact, they couldn't find a lie anywhere in their life together, but they genuinely missed their wedding. Its absence was the only incompleteness of their lives.

As active members of their local church and Sunday School teachers, they had long since resolved any theological misgivings. They had kept their vows and had discerned God's blessing on their life together. They never doubted God's love, or each others. The covenant between them had grown more sacred and profound with each passing year, but they genuinely and profoundly missed their wedding.

Finally they decided to reclaim what had been lost to whatever extent it was possible. As the 25th anniversary of their wedding day approached, they decided on the nature of that reclamation.

They told everybody they were going to relive their wedding day. They would go back to the church where they were married and get the preacher there to renew their vows with them. Then they would take their honeymoon trip again. And then, said their children, they would come home to a grand celebration just like before.

And so they did, only they got to town much earlier in the day than they had in 1961. This time they went to the courthouse first and arrived at the church, license in hand, just as I returned from lunch. And so, because the Senior Pastor was out of the office that day, I became part of their story.

Their telling of it was a ceremony of its own. They had clearly shared the details with each other many times. They took turns filling in the details the way siblings retell that favorite Christmas at grandmother's house when it snowed and snowed. Their telling it in the safety of my study was strangely beneficial to them, but it would not be complete until they emerged from the church as husband and wife.

I told them our chapel was available, and might be more suitable for a wedding of this size, but they declined it. They had imagined the main sanctuary and the main sanctuary it would be. So the three of us entered that sacred space on another warm, hopeful, June afternoon and stood before the high altar where they exchanged their vows.

At first it seemed strange, just the three of us, our voices echoing around the empty, holy space, but quickly it began to feel natural, even perfect. When we finished, and they kissed, emotion overtook us all.

I became invisible as they exchanged their vows, flaw-lessly repeating the words of the liturgy at my prompting; words of love they had been saying in one form or another since third grade. They didn't even know I was there.

They had come inside at last to be married in the church of their dreams, just as the dreams of their lives had already come to fruition all around them. I have measured every wedding since by theirs.

Tears of the Statue

In her remarkable book <u>Dakota</u>, Kathleen Norris shares the poem of a little girl she once taught:

> When my third snail died, I said,
> "I'm through with snails."
> But I didn't mean it.
> (p.190. 1993, Houghton Mifflin Company, New York)

That's just how I feel about churches. I'm through with churches, but I don't mean it.

In my denominational tradition, the bishop and cabinet of district superintendents meet annually to make the decisions about which clergy will serve what church. This system, like all the others, is imperfect.

As a result, I've served churches I didn't want to serve. I've served churches longer than I wanted to, but I've never left a church without a great sense of loss and plenty of emotion. A colleague once remarked that he would dearly love the church, if it just weren't for the people. And yet we both knew, even as we laughed, that the church *is* the people and that we even love the ones who don't love us. One really can love and hate the same people at the same time.

Lots of weird stuff happens when a preacher leaves a church. People you thought would cry buckets hardly seem upset. People you always wondered about suddenly seem brokenhearted.

The hearts of parishioners seem to turn outward at the beginning of a new pastorate, then inward, then outward again at the end. This final turning outward has a certain reserve to it, though, like family awaiting an expected death. Nobody wants to hurt any more than they already do, so everybody pulls back a bit. *Better save something for the new parsonage family. Better spare ourselves as best we can.*

Conversations that are really about grief, but don't sound like it, happen all over the place. The obvious fact that none of the relationships we have shared will ever be the same turns into silly talk about how we will stay in touch and maintain fellowship in spite of everything. Everybody knows nothing will ever be the same again, because nothing ever is, but denial is the music of leaving and we play on.

Folks that never took you to dinner before take you out and talk about your future as if they will be a part of it. (They will be, of course, but not in the ways that they imagine.) Folks that haven't been to worship reappear out of curiosity. Notes arrive: *I was so surprised to learn that . . . I was shocked and saddened to hear that you will be . . . I hope you know how much we are going to miss . . .*

And the preacher can't help but imagine the text of some notes that (graciously) don't arrive: *I've been praying for so long that God would take you away from here and now I understand that my prayers have been answered. Is moving day still scheduled for . . . I was so glad to hear that you are leaving that I ordered a keg and invited in the neighbors. I suspect that many are glad that you will no longer . . . Even if another church's loss is our gain, I must confess that I'm still mighty glad to hear that you are . . .*

And all of this continues right up to that last Sunday morning when worship tears down barriers like nothing else. I get in there and start that familiar service in that familiar place for the last time and my voice breaks. My heart breaks. I'm a mess all over the place.

I see it on the faces of others too. I scan the crowd like always and come across a face that's welling up with tears, and I look away in order to maintain my composure and just get through the service. But then I see another face and another. There is no safe place for my eyes to rest. The collective emotion of the moment just comes crashing down and there is no place to hide.

And who really wants to hide from moments of shared grief, shared joy, shared confusion, hard work, shared hope, shared prayer, shared faith, shared anger, shared love, and shared life anyway? I do, at least at that moment, because it's too much. Each person in the pew has his or her own experiences that they have shared with me; the baptism of their child or grandchild, or their wedding day, or their spouse's funeral. Perhaps some recall the new initiative we started from scratch, the weekend retreat we shared, an emotional moment of profession of faith, or a counseling session of particular pathos. But all the funerals, all the weddings, conversations, births, deaths, and moments, such moments, descend upon me en masse and I am quite literally overwhelmed. It is too much for me to bear, and yet I bear it, and go home and have lunch, and start thinking about the next parish. It's unnatural, inhuman, like any ongoing life in the face of insufferable grief.

On the particular, inhuman, insufferable, last worship service on the Sunday I left associate ministerhood forever, one face stood out from the others even though I really didn't know him. I don't know if anyone did, because he was larger than life.

As the owner and CEO of a large and very successful local business, he was among the most prominent citizens of the city. He was successful in every kind of way. He was respected, feared, and revered by everyone. He was both deferred to and loved by his family, and he seemed to love them very much in return and be quite proud of them.

Somehow they all arrived at worship at the same time most Sunday mornings, as if in a motorcade. A shiny black Jaguar, followed by a shiny black Mercedes, followed by a shiny black Porsche would roll into the circular driveway right by the front doors of the sanctuary just moments before 11:00 o'clock. Out of each would step another generation of the same family, all impeccably attired and self-possessed. I don't know how they managed such synchronicity, but it was wonderful to see them arrive.

When he, or any member of his family, left worship they always shook my hand and spoke briefly, each the picture of decorum appropriate to their generation. They had learned it from the family's patriarch. He knew how to behave in every situation.

I never officiated a wedding or funeral for him, or his loved ones. We never served on a committee together. He never attended Sunday School, or Bible Study, or Board

Meetings. He was absolved of these. He was above them, outside them, otherwise engaged.

And so we never had a conversation, not really, until the Saturday morning before my last Sunday. I was packing up the last of my study when he stopped by the church hoping to find me.

He entered my study without hesitation, closing the door behind him, and thus I beheld a man I had never met. He seemed older, vulnerable and ill at ease, so I immediately felt uncomfortable too.

He put out his hand and I took it, to shake I supposed, but we didn't really shake. He just stood there holding my hand and looking at me. Then his eyes welled up with tears and he said, *I won't attend the goodbye party later. I'm not good at that sort of thing. But I wanted to tell you face to face the difference you have made in my life. I am a different man because of your preaching. I am different in the way I handle my business. I am different as a person. I just wanted to thank you, and to wish you well.*

Somewhere during this speech I realized there was folded currency in the palm of his hand. It wasn't any great deal of money, especially for such a man, but it was a token, something he knew how to give by way of expressing himself. He let go of my hand turned and left, closing the door behind him.

This was not the most remarkable encounter I had in that study, but it ranks among them. I remember looking at the door he had just closed behind him and wondering what a person does next. What does a preacher do following such a moment? I think I walked to my now empty desk and sat behind it in a stupor, but I'm not sure.

That's why we preach. There is nothing more. A summit was achieved, an obstacle overcome, a great victory won, but no one was cheering. No trophy was presented. The preacher can't even tell anyone, except perhaps the long-suffering spouse and mine was too upset at the moment (from having her life turned upside down by another move) to hear, or much care. I was trying to move on to the next parish when this last astonishing word from the current parish was delivered, into the very midst and mess of my own suffering and loss, the lovely corner office I was exchanging for a converted bedroom in the country parsonage to which we were being sent.

A word of grace and encouragement had come crashing into my world of self pity and confusion. A word of grace had come and, as usual, found me unprepared.

A prodigal had come home as a result of my preaching, but this one had made his own inheritance. There was no older brother to hassle with and the fatted calf would live on. There would be no party except the one arranged for that evening to send me on my way feeling appreciated. We all had places to get to.

He was present at worship the next morning. His was one of the faces I scanned. He was composed and stoic as always. I wanted to shout, but didn't dare.

Jocks for Jesus

Following a very sincere prayer offered in and through Jesus Christ our Lord: a basketball player gets in the face of the volunteer official who just called the foul that put him out of the game, a preacher drills a young woman in the back with a softball, a grown man runs hard into a young, female catcher guarding home plate and knocks her ten feet onto the flat of her back.

Yep, we're talkin' ecclesiastical sports.

I've never experienced the church without sports. My Dad bowled on a church-league team for as long as he could. When I was a teenager, I played on our church basketball team. I credit that experience with teaching me enough about the game to become competitive. I still remember the phone call I made to our coach telling him I wouldn't be playing on the church team that year, because I would be playing for the junior varsity team at my high school. *I'm really proud of you,* he said. *I knew you could do it. We'll miss you, but I'm so glad you're getting this opportunity. You deserve it.*

He was a wonderful guy, our coach. He was in his late

twenties, had married one of the prettiest and nicest girls in our church, and had even played on the varsity basketball team at the nearby state university. Even though we played our church-league games in a run-down municipal gymnasium with shredded nets and a big bump in the middle of the court caused by some weird kind of warping in the floor, he rose above it. He glided up and down the court with athletic grace and an easy confidence that declared he could have his way with the opposing team. He could hold off the most rabid defender with one hand while dribbling dexterously with the other. Some defenders he would leave standing in their tracks as he faked one way and then swooped to the bucket the other. Others he simply went through.

He was humble and yet confident. He was warm and kind, but yet intimidating. He was my hero, and when my hero told me he was proud of me and that I deserved to make the junior varsity team, I felt fantastic.

My Dad's bowling teams and their genuine camaraderie, and my experience with the church basketball team as an adolescent, instilled in me a love for church-related sports. These experiences helped teach me the importance of community and how bonds could be forged within the church through mutual striving and teamwork. They did not, however, prepare me for certain other aspects of church athletics.

When, at my first appointment, I decided it would be good for the church to have a softball team, most everyone else agreed. It was good for us too, until we lost our first four games. I was OK with losing. I'm one of those strange people who actually enjoys playing the games so much that winning is simply a bonus that comes around once in a while. Most folks don't think this way.

After our third consecutive loss the boys and younger men at the church started bringing friends to worship; big friends, friends with a lean and hungry look, friends you wouldn't want to know in any other capacity. Immediately following worship, each friend was dutifully introduced to me as someone who wanted to play softball with us and who would be faithfully at worship the designated number times necessary to meet the requirements of the league we were in. It was all true. These friends almost always attended worship as promised and they never missed a softball game.

One of these friends, a man mountain named Daryl, weighed just over three hundred pounds, was renowned for helping local farmers get up hay by grasping three bales in each hand and tossing them onto the flatbed wagon like so many pillows, was otherwise employed as a bouncer for a roughneck bar across the river, and could hit a softball literally out of sight. The field where we played our games adjoined the local fire and rescue building and was mowed as far back as anyone could reasonably be expected to hit a baseball or a softball. When Daryl came to bat, opposing outfielders simply stood on the outermost edge of the mown area in the hope of following the ball's trajectory and eventually finding it in the weeds and brush. After the young men of the church assembled their friends, we didn't lose any more softball games and nobody on the other teams gave us any crap either.

It was while we were on this testosterone roll that it was brought to my attention that somebody knew of a young man who played minor-league hockey during the winter and liked speaking to church youth groups during the off season. Being the off season, this person wondered if we couldn't invite this faithful, young athlete to our church to speak. I couldn't think of any reason why not and so a few weeks later the hockey player stood in my pulpit one Sunday night and addressed a church about two thirds full of young people from five miles up and down the two-lane in either direction.

He started kind of clumsily, but soon got going and before he was done had pretty well used every cliché known to popular Christianity during thirty rambling minutes of witness. The only thing I remember from his talk was a reference to the tension between knocking the stuffing out of people on the ice and sharing the love of Jesus. He cried at one point and lots of others did too. When he was finished, he fielded questions from the kids.

One kid, apparently taken by the very issue that interested me, asked how it was that he could play a violent game like hockey and be a Christian at the same time. The young athlete explained that the violence of hockey is simply part of the game and that if you aren't willing to give as good as you get you can't be an effective player. That pretty much covered the hockey part and we all just sat there waiting for the Christian part until another kid asked another hockey question and things just rolled on from there.

Years later, during softball season at another church, I drilled a young woman in the back with a softball. She had made the fateful decision of rounding first base as if trying to stretch a single into a double. By the time she realized the error of her ways and turned back toward first, she had come so far that I thought I had a good chance of throwing her out. Hey, it was a playoff game! I only meant to throw her out, not hurt her, and anyway, the first baseman showed an especial lack of effort by not trying to reach around her for the ball and subsequent tag.

Later in the same game, a man on the opposing team tried to separate our female catcher from the ball as she stood holding it in her mitt and guarding home plate. He knocked her for a loop, but she held on and he was out. Hey, it was a playoff!

And there's the annual Methodist/Presbyterian golf tournament played at yet another church even more years later, after my softball playing days had clearly passed. Each year the Presbyterian minister and I tried to come up with ways of making the tournament more of a fun & fellowship, *let's raise some money for mission* event, and each year it became increasingly cutthroat with ringers, foot wedges, cursing and the like.

And there have been the church teams that all members of the church aren't welcome to play on, because they don't really bring anything to the table. And there was the time our church youth group was accused of bringing in a ringer to a District Youth Olympics, because a twenty-something former youth leader was visiting that weekend and wanted to re-connect with everybody and went along to the event and turned out to be a darned good volleyball player. And there's the time I wanted to strangle a parishioner of mine, because every serve he attempted in the volleyball game that could have gotten us into the playoffs was served squarely into the net because he was thinking of himself rather than the team.

We probably ought to declare the concept of church sports morally and theologically bankrupt and gather instead around activities that aren't about winning, losing or competing. There are certainly lots of good models out there, lots of group activities that promote teamwork without promoting a handful of physically gifted people to the head of the line and leaving others feeling resentful and second class.

But then there's *The Wave*, a group of twelve to fifteen older adults at one church who dearly loved watching church softball games. They brought their folding chairs to every game and placed them in a line near our team's bench. Every time we scored a run they would perform that classic stadium maneuver known as the wave. Except it was a little wave that started at one end of the folding chairs and rippled, or sure tried to, down the line to the end. They were *The Wave* and proud of it. Eventually they got matching t-shirts. *The Wave* had a lot of fun and brought joy to everyone present.

And there's that incredible round of golf that my son-in-law and I carded during one of the Methodist/Presbyterian blood lettings. I still remember some of those shots. I'll never forget the big smile on his face. It was something special that we did together, like the round of golf I had played with the Presbyterian minister a few weeks before. Ostensibly it was played to get us ready for the competition, but it turned out to be a time of intimacy and sharing that helped us become true friends.

And there're my Dad's bowling buddies, the ones who encouraged him when he was sick and about to give up on recuperation, the ones who said they would hold his place on the team no matter how long it took him to get back. (My Dad's bowling average was already in steady decline. They were not acting from a desire to win.)

And there's that phone call, the one I made to my hero years ago. *I'm really proud of you,* he said. *I knew you could do it. We will miss you, but I'm so glad you are getting this opportunity. You deserve it.* I'm not sure I'm willing to miss out on that, even for all the theological correctness in the world.

Joe Cool

The church, almost as much as the house I shared with my parents, was my home growing up, so many of my earliest recollections are set there. Ours was a beautiful neighborhood church of stone and stained glass. Because my father was handicapped and we didn't own a car until I was thirteen, we didn't get out much; so outside of school, the church (which was in walking distance of our house) was the center of my social life, especially in summer.

Sunday School and church were much-anticipated events, and pretty much whatever activity the church offered, I was there. One of my favorite summer activities was Vacation Bible School. As a child it was a time of socialization and fun. As a youth it was a time of helping (usually by supervising recreation) and interacting with my adolescent peers, especially girls.

One of these summers, the one between middle school and high school, was especially memorable. None of my group was old enough to drive, but we were sure old enough to want to. We wanted so many things, wondrous and exciting things.

And into that summer (as we washed cars in the church parking lot one sunny afternoon to raise money for some long-forgotten project and threw wet sponges at each other's fresh, young bodies) rolled Joe Cool in a white Triumph two-seater with the top down, his gear piled in the back, dark hair tousled by the wind, and sporting sunglasses just like Snoopy wore when posing as the very same guy. He was a divinity student from Duke University come for a summer internship at the church. The girls didn't look at anybody else the rest of the summer and my buddies and I were jealously in awe.

Joe Cool would live in the two-story brick house adjacent to the church that had stood empty since the last Associate Pastor left. It became a favorite destination that summer.

After shutting off the engine and getting out of the car, Joe walked right over and invited us guys to help him carry his gear into the house. Since it didn't take long for us to unload his Triumph, we were soon sitting around on the dusty furniture imagining with him where things ought to go and brainstorming about all the cool things we could do together there and did our best to answer his questions about grocery stores, burger joints, movie theaters, and other essential places. He told us to consider his place open pretty much around the clock.

After he was settled, he insisted upon taking us all home in gratitude for our services and pledges of further help and friendship. Though most of us lived within comfortable walking distance of our homes, we eagerly squeezed into his sports car. We were a moving traffic violation before we cleared the church parking lot and couldn't have cared less.

Joe wasn't at all concerned that a host of body parts hung dangerously over the edges of his car. He sped through the neighborhoods, motor revving and gears shifting. We were a pod full of ear-to-ear smiles. I remember wishing that everyone who knew me could see me in these glorious moments.

Not everybody took Joe up on his open house invitation, but I sure did. I spent hours sitting around there shooting the breeze. I always expected him to mention God at some point, but he never did. We just talked about stuff.

I didn't know what to think about that. I liked having Joe's attention and I liked having a cool older friend, but I wanted something more too. I think I needed the God talk that never came.

To complicate matters further, there was often beer in Joe's refrigerator. He never offered us any, but he never tried to hide it either. I often speculated about what he would do if we asked him for one. None of us ever got the courage.

To complicate matters even further, Joe had a girl-friend. He always made a point of preparing us well in advance when she was coming for a visit. She came three or four times that summer, always staying in the house with Joe the entire weekend. She was, of course, drop-dead gorgeous. They were such a striking couple they might have been movie stars. By way of preparing us for her stay, Joe explained that the open house policy would be amended during her visits. We were still welcome to come by, but only during the day and only after knocking and waiting on the porch for permission to enter.

That actually suited us fine. She was so beautiful, and we were still so inept around girls, especially beautiful ones, that we felt painfully awkward and ill at ease in her presence. She was smart too. She seemed to always be saying something clever and she seemed always to be trying to draw us into her spectacularly clever world. We weren't worthy, or ready, or anything but clumsy in her presence. When she was visiting, we kept our distance. Except for one situation I couldn't avoid.

I felt honored and uncomfortable all at the same time. On the morning of the church picnic Joe Cool invited me to ride with him and his girlfriend, who was visiting that weekend. (Joe recognized my loneliness, as well as my transparent admiration. I suppose one or both motivated him.) As fate would have it, however, our minister and his wife asked Joe and his girlfriend to ride with them and we were all stuck. I rode in the backseat of our minister's big sedan with the beautiful couple, her lovely self, seated between Joe and me, with the Rev. Thomas and his wife up front.

I was so nervous I could hardly breathe. I can still smell her scent and feel her smooth thigh against mine. I can still remember what her hair felt like brushing against my face as she flipped her head from side to side, and I can still feel the tension in that car, a tension that seemed to make the otherwise kindly Thomas's appear serious and stern, and which incited Joe and his girlfriend to act out.

The Rev. Thomas tried to make conversation with Joe, who surprised me by responding with something flip, and to my thinking, disrespectful. Mrs. Thomas tried to make conversation with Joe's girlfriend who followed Joe's example. I wasn't on anybody's radar until Joe decided to include me in the festivities.

Joe leaned over to his girlfriend and whispered something in her ear that caused her to laugh out loud. She turned to me and whispered the same in my ear. (Did I mention that I can still remember her hair brushing against my face?) *Didn't I think, (Joe wanted to know), that the Rev. Thomas's sport shirt looked like he had forgotten to change out of his pajamas?* Yes, in fact, I did, but I hadn't noticed, or thought much about it until that moment. I chuckled softly, because she and Joe wanted me to, but I didn't like how it made me feel and it sure didn't reduce the tension in that car. Then Joe started the whole chain of events over again by wondering *if Mrs. Thomas' hair didn't look like something a swarm of hornets might fly out of any second.*

It was one long ride to the picnic. I got a ride home with a friend and his parents. Things were never quite the same with Joe and me. Lots of things changed for me that summer, lots of things that never changed back. Questions arose that I'm still trying to answer:

Why does image hold such power over people, especially the young?

Why does the church expend so much energy enforcing relatively unimportant mores while stoically tolerating truly hurtful behavior?

Why do the most seductive and alluring things come up short in the end?

Why are good and evil, right and wrong, so difficult to isolate, so tightly braided into the knot of human pathos?

What is that dream we all still chase, the one my friends and I glimpsed that long ago summer afternoon in a white Triumph?

Chapter Two:

IN THE FACE OF DEATH

White Lightnin'

Ihad been clergy less than 24 hours. Surely God would wait until I matriculated at seminary before sweeping me into the powerful currents of life's mighty river. Surely God could hold off sending me a wedding, or a funeral, or some besieged soul wrestling with heaven and hell, sin and death. Surely God would wait until my wife and I unpacked the boxes labeled "kitchen," would wait until we got our little daughters settled in their new (and already unhappily shared) bedroom.

The God who had called (*blasted* is more like it) me from quiet mediocrity, plucked me from the tree of comfort and calm and unceremoniously repotted me in this odd and unfamiliar place masquerading as our new home, this God would never dump burdens upon me that would make a veteran shudder.

Yes and no.

The phone call heralding my first funeral didn't come from a bereaved family member, or an unctuous funeral director, but from the gentle man who had pastored my new flock for three years prior to my arrival. I simultaneously learned that a funeral was required and that, with my permission of course, he would lead the service.

It's **one** of the strange things about ministers that even those so new to their turf that they can barely identify it, bristle at sharing it. A burden I could not have borne was being carried for me in love, and still I bristled. There was more though.

I didn't want to admit what was obvious to everyone but me. I didn't want to admit to being tentative and incompetent. I had, after all, successfully completed 2 entire weeks of denominational training as something called a "local pastor." (Being trained as a local pastor is kind of like local anesthesia. One's sphere of influence is contained by design.)

My predecessor offered to pick me up for what I instantly learned was the obligatory visit to the funeral parlor. He filled me in on the way over in his car. *A very tragic story*, he said.

Forty-nine years before, a judge had sentenced an 18-year-old youth to 40 years in prison. All forty years had been duly served. Age 18 going in. Age 58 coming out.

The young man had gone hunting with his 17-year-old cousin and a jar of white lightnin'. Their youth, the shared jar, and their loaded weapons had proved a deadly combination. The 18-year-old couldn't really say what had happened for certain, except he sure never meant to shoot his cousin. *Forty years,* Said the judge, and that was that.

I visited him a few times, my predecessor reflected. *He hardly said a word, just sat there in a rocking chair on the front porch chain smoking and rocking. Some family took him in. They said he seemed to love their kids and the dog. Seemed to love just being there watching their lives. Seemed like a gentle soul. Sad. Really sad.*

He was laid out in a small, dimly lit visitation room in the township funeral parlor, an old-fashioned place clinging to the side of a steep hill. Two freestanding lamps at either end of the casket looked as if they had been fashioned in some gray, northeastern city about the time the deceased started serving his sentence. The light they produced was so wan and reluctant that it bore scant resemblance to anything truly luminous. No one had signed the guest book. The undertaker, my predecessor and I were the only ones present besides the corpse.

We stood there in awkward silence for a few brief moments. Then my predecessor and the funeral director chatted briefly about the logistics of the service on the following day.

In at 18. Out at 58. 9 quiet years on the porch.

My predecessor said some kind words at graveside the next day. I read some scripture sentences and a prayer from my brand new *Book of Worship.* When we were done the handful of people in attendance quietly dispersed. My predecessor graciously thanked me for my help.

During his remarks, I had imagined some of the cast of characters from the deceased man's life. Where was the judge? In a long-term care facility in Florida, or greeting friends in resurrection? Where were the court-appointed attorney and the probation officer of today? Where were the young woman and children of his own, his own dog for his own porch?

His name was John Smith. No kidding. Only John Doe, I suppose, would have been more fitting.

He died of lung cancer, and other things.

How Many Psalms?

*T*he *New Oxford Annotated Bible with The Apocrypha (Revised Standard Version)* contains 151 psalms. Otherwise, there is a nice round 150. But how many are there *really*?

For the elderly gentleman who grilled me on the subject, there were 150. He wasn't an apocryphal kind of guy.

I never knew Mason when he could walk. I saw him stand with difficulty. I saw him shuffle his feet behind his walker in order to get from his wheelchair to his favorite chair, or from his bed to his wheelchair, but I never saw him at full function, except through my imagination when his wife and neighbors told stories of him.

Apparently he was a pistol most all his life. He worked harder and longer than most. He was more opinionated and outspoken than most. Men often disagreed with or disapproved of Mason, but they admired him in the way men just naturally admire strength, stamina and guts. Women avoided him and rolled their eyes when speaking of his exploits. Everyone agreed that he was a handful. Everyone agreed that he loved his wife, his country, Jesus, and his church.

He'd had his first stroke before I became his minister. He had the most devastating one shortly thereafter. He was my first protracted pastoral care experience.

I visited him in the hospital and after he returned home. Since his "recovery" was lengthy, I witnessed the arduous, incomplete return of his hands, legs and speech.

His wife, whose unflappable southern gentility never effectively concealed her steely strength, cared for him throughout. She never ceased reminding me how much Mason appreciated my visits. I was never sure which of those two appreciated them most, and it never mattered, except as I struggled to figure out what they most needed.

It wasn't my prayers, because these felt anemic to me in the omnipresence of the effects of a stroke. It wasn't my easy ecclesiastical charm, because I was, at that point in my career, without any. I hope I have come to better understand what they needed, and in retrospect I suppose I supplied it even then in some fashion, perhaps making up with earnestness what I lacked in ability. Whatever the case, they loved me well and seemed to genuinely cherish my visits.

I learned, over time, *the* event of their lives, the loss of their only child. They knew from the beginning that he had a bad heart. They knew that his life would be short, but they were nevertheless, as are we always, devastated by the news that he had collapsed and died on the school playground at the age of 13.

They never told the story, or even spoke of it, in each other's presence. Each told me the story from her or his perspective, ONCE. And yet, this was their story more than their financial good fortune, or their successful and doting nieces and nephews, or anything else in all creation. Their love had become flesh and lived among them for 13 years and had died.

Mason had been less talkative than usual on this particular visit. I wasn't sure if he was unable or unwilling. I'd carried the conversation along, but wasn't proud of it. I had almost exhausted my personal reflections on the weather, when Mason broke his silence to ask me how many psalms there are.

He didn't ask the way a teacher asks a class for the square root of 64, or the way a coach asks his linemen how it is that they aren't blocking. He asked the way one person asks another if they saw last night's sunset. "Do you know how many psalms there are?"

I didn't, and I was embarrassed that I didn't. A man's minister had come to bring holy comfort and didn't know how many psalms there are.

I have revisited that moment many times, not as a moment of humiliation, but as a moment of grace. I still see Mason sitting across from me in his wheelchair, a cotton throw across his nearly useless legs, his eyes resting gently but unwaveringly on mine. "There are 150," he said. Then he repeated it, slowly, with emphasis on each word. "There are 150 psalms."

We both understood that he was offering me a gift, that he was opening himself to me as never before. Mason was letting me know the power and sustenance of the Psalms. This old straight shooter was letting me know what staying power the Psalms had, a staying power he relied upon and that I'd better keep in my arsenal too.

Mason gave me the psalms that day, **_all_** of them. He especially gave me the ones I didn't like because they are so searingly real:

My soul is full of troubles . . . How long, O LORD? Will you hide yourself forever? . . . I am like a lonely bird on the housetop. All day long my enemies taunt me; those who deride me use my name for a curse. For I eat ashes like bread, and mingle tears with my drink because of your indignation and anger; for you have lifted me up and thrown me aside. . . Like arrows in the hand of a warrior are the sons of one's youth . . . For I am poor and needy, and my heart is pierced within me. . . You have kept count of my tossings; put my tears in your bottle. Are they not in your record?

And of course, *Blessed is the one who comes in the name of the LORD*, even if he doesn't yet know how many psalms there are.

Suitable Clothes

Mary Sue came to us incrementally. At first she came to the church for food, clothing, rent, or help with bills. She kept coming for these things, but also and increasingly for community. She found among the church staff something new to her, people who listened and seemed to care.

Mary Sue was barely five feet tall and weighed less than 100 pounds, but everybody else in her life was big. The men who sometimes came with her were big, rough-looking fellows. Her daughter, who also accompanied her on occasion, was an imposing presence as well. Occasionally one of the men, or the daughter, came on their own but not for conversation. They made their requests and moved on.

Mary Sue was different. Mary Sue wanted something more.

Eventually, she asked one of us if it would be OK if she came to church some Sunday. We assured her that it would and she came the very next.

Mary Sue was one of those people that just gets to you.

She was a study in poverty and hard living, and getting herself fixed up for Sunday worship somehow accentuated this. Only once did I see her wearing clothes that fit. Clothes just hung on her in the most unattractive way. Mary Sue was weather-beaten, and sometimes bruised.

She appeared to be in her late forties, but it's difficult to tell the age of a woman whose life has been that hard. She reminded me of the Appalachian women in those black and white photographs taken in the early part of the previous century who looked forty while still in their teens. She was, however, a woman in her fifties and thus older than she looked. Her slight frame and innate spryness disguised her age.

Mary Sue would talk to you if you tried, but nothing about her made anybody want to try. Some of the ladies and men did try too, God love them. They tried to carry on polite conversation with Mary Sue during refreshment time. Some even invited her to go with them to their Sunday School class. All of the staff greeted her and called her by name, but nothing much came of it conversationally. Mary Sue was never "fine," or interested in the weather. When one of the well-meaning ladies complimented her on a dress she was wearing for the first time she ignored them. She knew what she looked like and didn't care to talk about it.

Mary Sue just didn't have anything to say that anybody wanted to hear. She was that honest and her life was that bad. I've never heard someone discuss being thrown out of her apartment, or being physically, sexually, or psychologically abused, or being painfully hungry or disgustingly sick, during refreshment time at church, and that's about all Mary Sue had to talk about besides her genuine thankfulness for all the ways the church had helped her. Because she believed that help ultimately came from God, her presence at Sunday worship was her way of saying *Thank You* to God.

So Mary Sue became a fixture at Sunday worship. She was never a part of things in the conventional sense, but managed to carve out a place for herself. She was Mary Sue, that sad, strange little woman you can't really talk to. She stood all alone, holding her Dixie Cup of lemonade, amid the buzz and bustle of refreshment time; a remote island that didn't seem to mind being an island all that much.

Mary Sue attended worship regularly for about a year and during that time things slowly improved for her. Her daughter found a man that treated her well and at their invitation Mary Sue moved in with them. Things were going better for everybody. Mary Sue decided she was ready to join the church.

After meeting with both the church's ministers to make certain it was unanimously OK for her to become a member, Mary Sue felt sufficiently comfortable to allow us to set a date for her joining. She had never been baptized and so her entry into the church was shaping up as a pretty big day.

Her last request to us was for a brand new, store-bought dress suitable for her baptism. I've long been a proponent of more casual dress for worship. It just seems to make things easier for everybody and I'm convinced God isn't a bit fashion conscious, but something about Mary Sue's insistence on a new dress moved me deeply.

It wasn't about fashion. It wasn't about vanity. It wasn't about fitting in, or passing muster, or anything except pleasing God. The God to whom Mary Sue was saying "Thank You" deserved better than anything Mary Sue had in her closet, or could acquire on her own. God deserved a brand new, store bought dress and she wasn't taking "no" for an answer.

A lady on the church staff went shopping with Mary Sue and helped her pick out her dress, paying for it and a pair of matching shoes after Mary Sue agreed that both were right for the occasion. They chose well. On her special Sunday, Mary Sue looked nice. She didn't look lovely, or beautiful, or attractive, and she didn't look like somebody who fit in, but she really looked nice. Mary Sue was shined up like a new penny. She sat on the very front row that Sunday along with her daughter and her daughter's boyfriend.

As the service unfolded, the time finally came for Mary Sue's official grafting into the church. The Senior Minister and I walked ceremoniously to the center of the sanctuary and stood with the high altar behind us, the baptismal font open and expectant between us, and a semicircle of polished wooden kneelers with gorgeously embroidered cushions in front of us. We invited Mary Sue and her family to join us in that auspicious space. As they came forward and Mary Sue walked toward us, I noticed tears in the eyes of some in the congregation and smiles of genuine love from many others. The Senior Minister and I worked carefully through the liturgy, like high wire artists wrestling with a critical, delicate balance. We wanted it to be gentle and genuine and good. Mary Sue performed admirably, though I'm not sure she was paying that much attention to our words.

Finally the moment came for her baptism and the Senior Minister asked her to please kneel for the sacrament.

But instead of kneeling, Mary Sue stepped up onto one of the beautiful, embroidered kneeling cushions and stood there proud and erect in her new dress and matching shoes, looking heavenward. She looked like one of those ladies on the prow of a ship, head thrown back as if inviting the wind to do its darnedest, all the while knowing she would prevail against it.

A collective taking-in of breath occurred when Mary Sue stepped up onto the kneeler. People were shocked, surprised, worried that things would get out of hand, dismayed, embarrassed for Mary Sue, and horrified at the thought of anybody's shoes standing on one of those beautiful kneelers that had been so painstakingly embroidered and were so carefully protected.

The taking in of breath was followed by an awkward silence. "Please step down." The Senior Minister said quietly. She stood resolute.

"Mary Sue, please step down." He repeated. At this point I motioned to the kneeling cushion as if to point the way. Then we both motioned. A few more difficult seconds passed and Mary Sue stepped down.

"Please kneel, Mary Sue." The Senior Minister said.

Mary Sue just stood there. She was now genuinely confused. It had never occurred to us to talk with her about the logistics of baptism, just as it had never occurred to her that it could happen any other way than with herself standing as tall and straight and high as possible while looking heavenward, right into the face of God.

Mary Sue was baptized standing up. She tilted her head forward just a bit as our hands, dripping water, started toward her.

A few weeks after her baptism, Mary Sue became seriously ill. She was diagnosed with cancer and given a short
lease. In my last visit to her in the hospital she told me that
she would "never forget" the occasion of her baptism, so
special was that day to her, and so precious.

The image of Mary Sue standing before that large and
privileged congregation looking like a lady on the prow
of a majestic sailing ship and wearing the only outfit that
was probably ever hers alone in this life, burnt itself into
my mind and heart. I knew it then, and have known it ever
since. Mary Sue was the one who truly fit in that day. The
rest of us are still learning how we want to be before God
and each other, still searching for what we really want to say
during refreshment time.

Swept Away

Imet her on the first day of my new appointment as the Associate Minister of a large church. We were friends thereafter. She never attended worship, or visited the church grounds during my three years as one of her ministers, but her friendship was a constant blessing.

I would be bolstered by her friendship and her prayers, even though I didn't imagine needing bolstering as I walked to the hospital from my carpeted, corner office that bright July afternoon. Striding brick sidewalks beneath huge oaks, I passed the stately homes of the city's most prosperous families. If I didn't look cocksure and purposeful in my best shoes and only summer suit, it wasn't from lack of trying.

There were often ten or twelve people on this church's hospital list. They were visited daily by the Senior Minister or me. We visited on alternating days, handing off the card bearing their names as if playing a twisted game of hot potato. We couldn't be rid of it fast enough and yet we passed that card back and forth with studied words of pastoral concern and collegiality. "Poor Mr. So-n-so is certainly dwindling isn't he? And little Mrs. What's-her-name, isn't she a cat bird?"

A simple *Go with God* would have better served us both. Despite our daily ceremony, we more nearly resembled two pack mules whose master mercifully moves the load from one to the other as they soldier up a mountain.

Except it was my first day on the new job. I hadn't become that pack mule yet. In fact, I was exhilarated.

My seminary training had taught me that each encounter is an opportunity for contact with mystery and holiness, for significant and powerful pastoral ministry. Too soon, however, the routine of parish life finds one treating those encounters like a pile of rocks that need moving across the yard. You just hike up your britches and get to it. When the mystery and holiness happen, you are more surprised than anybody.

Except, like I said, it was my first day on the job and my first time in this particular hospital. It was one of the old-fashioned, mid-twentieth century kinds of hospitals that have long since given way to larger, brighter facilities with more glass, wider hallways and plenty of parking. It had wards, and metal-railed beds, and tiny single rooms tucked here and there that seemed more like pantries than places of healing and modern medicine.

Lydia was in one of the pantries, just lying there looking up at the ceiling obviously disgusted with the whole thing. Because her room was so small and ill-suited to house a person in a bed, she was visible to anyone in the long hallway looking in her direction. Closing or opening the door meant choosing between claustrophobia and public humiliation. She had chosen the latter.

She turned her head to see who, or what was coming, and gave me a look of "What now?" as I stood in her doorway.

And who might you be? She asked with no small amount of challenge in her voice.

I'm your new preacher, I answered, with just a hint of sass.

You don't look old enough to be my preacher. She said, with a *don't get cheeky with me boy* edge to her voice. I figured she must be a teacher and it turned out she was, but of the retired variety.

How are you feeling? I asked more respectfully.

Not well enough to go home, but I'm working on it. So tell me about you. According to the newsletter you're married with two daughters.

And on we went with me supplying whatever details she asked for and her revealing nothing. To this day I don't know why she was in the hospital then, or ever, and I never learned what her physical ailments were. These things bored her so much that she couldn't bear to waste life's precious moments talking of them.

Lydia was in her late seventies and thin as a rail. Her hair was still dark. If she colored it she did a nice job. Our relationship was one long flirtation that we both thoroughly enjoyed. Without the possibility of an actual romance we were free to enjoy one another's company without guilt of any kind and we did.

Her husband, and the love of her life, had died eight years before and much of her had died with him. Our friendship revived some of her lost self. She told me several times that

I reminded her of him. Mostly I think it was the fact that I thought she was so neat.

The hospitalization, during which I first met her, lasted just long enough for us to begin a friendship, and for her to extract my assurance of frequent visits to her home when she got out. She lived in the apartment she and her husband had shared for over forty years. Without children of their own, they had never outgrown it nor thought of a reason to move.

It was filled with nice but aging furniture, carefully selected artifacts, and photos of the two of them. It was a place of good conversation, peace, joy and unwavering mutual affection.

My visits to her were ostensibly for her benefit and the benefit of the kingdom, or the community of faith, or however one might choose to put it. They were, in fact, for me. She knew this better than I did. I visited her when I needed to be in that place of good conversation, peace, joy and unwavering mutual affection.

I've encountered most of the possible forms of disappointment and frustration in the homebound. Some come right out and lambaste you for coming so seldom. I prefer this variety. I appreciate the honesty of these folks and don't much blame them for feeling as they do.

The passive aggressive ones are more difficult. One little lady was always sweet as could be throughout our visit, but at the very end, when I would close with a prayer, she would continue with a prayer of her own until she got all her frustrations out. Her additions pretty much ruined the hymn *Sweet Hour of Prayer* for me.

Others revealed their anger throughout the visit, usually beginning with a cool reception followed by a tear here, a break in the voice there, and/or going on about all the OTHER ministers who visited so much more frequently (their daughter's minister, their neighbor's minister, their grandson's minister, their nephew's minister, etc.). Another popular device was the detailed litany of former ministers who came so faithfully, and with whom they enjoyed such a wonderful, intimate relationship. These folks always genuinely wondered why they didn't get visited more often.

Lydia knew all of this and she liked teasing me about it. She started by asking me if I had heard the saying about what the road to Hell is paved with. She assured me that I had laid quite a highway for myself where she was concerned. Every time I visited she described it for me. It had been paved many times. It had rest areas, freshly painted lines, wide shoulders and ran for thousands of miles.

So I always visited her last, following an afternoon of the other kinds of visits. She was my reward and I always left plenty of time for her, because I knew I would spend a much better evening at home as a result. She looked at me with sheer delight and a sparkle in her eyes as I spilled my guts about whatever.

When my three year tour of duty as an Associate Minister was about over, and it became known that I was being appointed to another parish, a new element was interjected into our visits, discomfort. Our free and easy way of relating grew strained. My leaving loomed over everything.

Our last visit was difficult and awkward. Our relationship had been built on sarcasm and delight in the foibles of others. Now our own foibles got in the way. We wanted to speak honestly of our feelings, but we hadn't laid the groundwork. It wasn't a warm or satisfying moment, but we both wished it was.

So time and life did their number on us. I went to my new parish and became consumed by it and she went on quietly living in her apartment and not being visited enough by the clergy and missing her husband and I guess me too sometimes.

But this isn't about sadness and loss, it's about the resulting punishment. It's about the myriad ways we punish others, and especially ourselves, because life is so filled with sadness and loss, as if these alone weren't sufficient to wreck us. It's about how the lonely punish those who finally do come. It's about how those who finally do come punish themselves for not arriving sooner. It's about how all of this begins in sadness and loss, but doesn't have to end there.

Lydia died less than a year after I left. I had mailed her a short note a couple of months earlier thanking her for her friendship, apologizing for not visiting her nearly enough, and wondering if my road to Hell had finally been closed.

A week later I received a card from her in reply. It wasn't a Hallmark card, because she wasn't a Hallmark kind of lady. It was a funny card with two goofy cartoon characters on the front; a white duck sitting on a little stool wearing a blue shirt and cap and blue flip flops and a brown bear standing behind him wearing a red and white striped t-shirt and holding his hands over the duck's eyes. At the top of the card is printed *Guess Who* - and inside is printed – *says Hi!*

Inside she wrote, *Sorry I can't write a real letter. Thanks for your letter – just want you to know "your pavement" is swept away! God Bless – Lydia.* What if we could all admit to being silly cartoon characters at best, and just bask in the forgiveness and love we've so slathered with cliché but never managed to grasp?

Chapter Three:

MYSTERY

The Holy Ghost

I'm kind of like Jimmy Buffett, *vampires, mummies and the holy ghost*, are among the things that *terrify me the most*. As a boy growing up in the church, I was always creeped out by the phrase, *Holy Ghost*. Even as an adult, I have been ever so thankful for its replacement with *Holy Spirit*.

This is because THE religious story of my life involves the Holy Ghost, at least that's the way my Mother tells it. I once went looking for the place of that awesome visitation, the spot where my Mother, and (by default) I, encountered God. I went looking, but I didn't realize it.

I was attending a ministers' conference in a small, southern Virginia town. Never having been much on ministers' conferences, I had spent the whole way down in the car wondering why I had bothered with this one.

Still wondering as I checked in at the conference center, I dropped off my suitcase and set out to explore the area, soon discovering an antique Army base. Since the gates were unguarded, I just drove in. Except for a lone vehicle parked here and there, the place was deserted. The out-of-date buildings and nearly-deserted landscape gave me the feeling I had entered a *Twilight Zone*.

In truth, however, roughly four decades after the fact, I had returned to the site of my life's determining. Subconsciously I must have known what I was doing, where I was going, but it only entered my consciousness as I drove among those eerie, empty buildings. I had come to the place where my family's life had been irrevocably altered.

On a bitterly cold, November night almost 40 years before, as my father returned to this army base after Thanksgiving, he was critically injured in an automobile accident. He and my mother, anticipating their first anniversary in a few weeks, feared he would be sent to Korea before they could celebrate it. Instead, he was to fight a much longer, and for him and us more devastating, war.

The young soldier who was driving that night fell asleep just minutes from the gates through which I had just passed. My father, already asleep in the back seat, was mangled in the wreckage, his head sustaining the most traumatic injuries. A doctor said my father would have bled to death beside the highway that night if it hadn't been so cold. Slight consolation, as little hope was offered for his survival and none for a return to normal life. My mother, with me six months along inside her, spent the next 5 weeks at the army base, alternating her time between sitting by my father's hospital bed, eating and resting just enough to keep us both alive, and praying; most of all, praying. During one of those periods of prayer, she encountered the Holy Ghost.

As pretty much the only female on an army base, she still didn't feel comfortable, even after several weeks, but she wasn't as fearful and ill at ease as she had been initially.

She had developed something of a routine, making daily rounds among the small room the army had provided, my Father's hospital bed, and the chapel. She always made the last round well after dark.

On this particular night she was especially weary, so weary in fact that when she entered the small chapel to pray (the last stop of the evening before returning to her room), she didn't even bother to turn on the lights, just collapsed in despair. She had been there only a moment, however, when she realized she wasn't alone. She was frightened by the overwhelming sense of someone very close. Who had been watching her? How many people knew her nightly routine? How could she have been so foolish?

Just as suddenly, however, she was overcome by a profound sense of well-being. The certainty that another living being was present never diminished. She simply stopped being afraid. She felt hope and life flow into her and she heard (in whatever way we hear such things) a reassuring, male voice telling her that everything was *going to be alright.*

Then, just as surely as she had known someone was there, she realized she was alone. She never did turn on the lights. After discerning the nature of the other, she felt no need.

In some ways, nothing would ever be alright for any of us again. My father had been destroyed in the accident and a handicapped stranger with a limited future left in his place. He gradually returned to life, but his essential self was gone. The young man one semester from his degree in pharmacy, drafted away from his studies to bolster the effort in Korea, was lost.

The life my mother had anticipated was suddenly replaced by a life no one would choose and few could bear. I would never really know my father, except through the words of those who knew him "before."

In other ways, though, everything was alright. My father lived, I was born healthy, veteran's benefits kept us going, and our three lives were grafted forever to that encounter between my mother and the Holy Ghost. Her life's determination and purpose, and by extension my own, were forged in the crucible of that moment.

As I drove around the army base that day, I looked for the hospital and the chapel, the specific buildings so crucial to my history, but if they still existed their usage had been altered or their signs removed. I only knew this was the place where it happened. There was no epiphany, only the certainty of that long-ago encounter and the knowledge of how it had affected me.

I write this on the threshold of Father's Day, 2003. I'll visit my Father on Sunday. Then, as a thousand times before, I'll try to discern something new, to discover that personal Rosetta stone that makes sense of it all. I once egocentrically speculated that he might have healed more people, more lastingly, through my ministry, than he would have in his career as a pharmacist; a most jejune deduction. God's ways are more mysterious, and God far more charitable than that. I would never have sacrificed my father's life and future for my own and neither would God.

Sometimes, when I'm with my Father, a word, a gesture, or a smile, like a shard of light suddenly introduced into a dark room, will startle me with the feeling that his true self is shining through. Sometimes, in a word, gesture, or smile of my own, I think I sense his light shining inside of me, pointing me in his direction.

For me, it comes down to fathers and sons. I will look for my Father until I find him, clinging all the while to another tragic Father and Son story that also turned out alright.

The Power of Touch

Having just left my wife in a hospital across town, I stood in the lobby of another hospital, one with a neonatal intensive care unit, looking for the admitting area. I needed to admit our newborn daughter, and then I needed to find her. I've never been more afraid. I believed my wife would survive, but feared that our daughter would not.

Early in the pregnancy, my wife *just knew* something wasn't right. That something was *placenta previa*, a condition in which the placenta forms abnormally across the uterus. We learned of it the night of her first hemorrhage, a hemorrhage so severe that we thought she was having a miscarriage. She spent the next two months at total bed rest, because the slightest movement could incite another hemorrhage.

Twice more during those long, worrisome weeks a hemorrhage took us back to the hospital. The third time, the doctors said enough was enough. My wife could take no more and the baby would be taken by emergency cesarean.

Because she was already anemic and now hemorrhaging again, Beth's trip to the operating room was like one of those television medical dramas with doctors and nurses racing her gurney down the hospital corridor tying up the loose ends of their gowns as they went. I ran with them, and just before they peeled me off at the O.R. doors, I asked the doctor if the baby was going to be alright. All he said, and that rather curtly, was that they were working to save my wife.

Almost two hours later the doctor informed me that she had tolerated the surgery well and that I could see her soon. He said the baby was struggling and was being prepared for transport to another hospital better equipped to meet her pressing needs. A daughter, I had another daughter, who might not survive.

I waited until I saw Beth safely in a room before leaving. She had already been informed of everything and urged me to the other hospital and whatever needed doing for our baby. It was almost 11:00 P.M. in late November. Anxious and afraid, I drove the dark miles between hospitals in a pouring rain. In such moments we experience an otherwise distant clarity, revealing both the amazingly few things that truly matter, and the visceral power these few things possess.

When I reached the other hospital's lobby, I was torn between finding our daughter and going to admitting for the necessary paperwork. Doing as I had been told, I went to admitting. When we were done, a woman there gave me directions to the neonatal intensive care unit.

I had already seen our daughter once, briefly, as doctors and nurses at her birth hospital frantically attached what seemed like dozens of tubes to two pounds of flesh. I had seen her tiny extremities through the gaps that occasionally opened among them as they worked over and around her. I had seen her heaving chest, fighting for every breath. I wasn't sure I could bear to see more. I feared that she might be struggling even more severely, or not struggling at all.

When I arrived at the doors of the unit and announced my presence through an intercom, a doctor soon appeared and explained things to me. Our daughter was now settled in what would be her home for the next two months. Her condition was simple, born too soon and with tiny membranes where tiny lungs should have been. He was a kind man and assured me that she just might make it. He would do his best.

He asked me if I would like to see her and I said *no*. He seemed surprised, but understanding. The nurse standing behind him wasn't as understanding. *Come in and see your daughter*, she said rather sternly. But I couldn't do it. I told her so and abruptly left, informing her I would be back the following morning. I was afraid my daughter was going to die and I didn't believe I could bear getting any more attached.

In order to improve our daughter's chance of survival, my wife pumped breast milk at her hospital every morning. We timed things so that I arrived at the hospital each morning about the time she was finished pumping. I then transported the fresh milk to the baby's hospital. The morning of my first delivery, as a nurse in the neonatal unit took the container of milk from me, she asked if I wanted to come in and see my daughter. *No*, I said, *I have to get to work*. (I wasn't a minister in those days.) After work, I visited Beth until the end of visiting hours and went straight home.

The following morning, when I made the milk drop at our daughter's hospital, a different nurse came to the door of the unit. As I handed over the milk, her hand bypassed the proffered parcel grabbing my wrist instead. *Come in,* she said. *Come in and see your daughter.* It wasn't a gentle grab. She latched onto my wrist with an iron grip. I was going into that unit. I was going to see my daughter.

Where is she? I asked as she pulled me in and closed the door firmly behind us. I looked around at a host of nurses, tiny babies in incubators, and medical equipment. The faces of all the nurses told me they were in cahoots. *Go over there and wash up,* the iron nurse said in response to my question. *You will want to reach in and touch her.*

I don't want to touch her. I'll just see her.

Go wash your hands.

Those nurses seemed prepared to move me to the sink and wash my hands for me if I hesitated much longer. I did as I was told.

So there I stood, next to our daughter's incubator. There were still lots of tubes, and she was still breathing hard, but not with the same difficulty as before. She seemed more peaceful. She lay on her back, little arms and legs spread out to both sides with her head facing away from me. The nurse, the iron nurse, bent down next to one of the little holes in the incubator and said in the kindest, sweetest voice, *Katherine, your Daddy's here.* And then she stepped back and away. (The nurse was thus the first person to attach the name we had chosen for a girl to the person we had been generically referring to as *the baby.*)

It seemed that we were alone now in all the world, Katherine and I. I loved her with all my heart.

Reach in and touch her, said a voice from behind me. *Go ahead, it's OK.*

I bent down and reached my hand through one of the little holes in the side of the incubator. As I did, Katherine turned her head toward me, wrapped the teensy fingers of her tiny hand as far around my index finger as they would go, and smiled.

She smiled!

I heard a collective gasp from the array of nurses hovering behind me. Even they were startled, and as moved and amazed as I. I was overwhelmed by a sense of well-being and hope. I felt surrounded by love. I was not comforting Katherine, she was comforting me. I was being comforted, by my tiny daughter, those nurses, and God.

That night, when visiting with my wife, I related as best I could what had transpired. She shared that she too had felt an overwhelming sense of hope and confidence in Katherine's future all day. She was moved but not really surprised by my story.

I arrived home late to the sound of our phone ringing. It was a friend and coworker who simply wanted me to know that everybody at work was thinking of us and praying for us. I can still hear the hope and strength in his closing words to me that night, words spoken almost thirty years ago; *I just know everything's going to be O.K. Yes,* I replied, *I believe it too.*

The next day, Katherine's doctor informed us that literally overnight membranes had become lungs. He was encouraged. Many difficult hurdles lay ahead, but her chances of survival were greatly improved.

God's commanding touch can be so delicate in application, so unlikely in source, so incomprehensible for all its specificity.

Grapes

Exorcisms are still performed, demons still cast out. I know. I was there.

My seminary required a semester of C.P.E. (Clinical Pastoral Education). I took mine at a hospital in Washington, D.C. and was fortunate indeed to be under the supervision of a particularly exceptional and experienced chaplain.

Having provided pastoral care for decades, he was adept both at giving pastoral care and teaching others to do so. Among the many beautiful gifts he gave us was his initial assignment to us aspiring clergy. He told us to walk every hospital corridor in which we were about to visit and *take the emotional temperature*. Only after passing through the length of a corridor could we enter a specific room, there to continue taking the temperature and begin our work. Right away he wanted us to attune ourselves to the emotional atmosphere around us, an atmosphere that included visitors, staff and patients. He wanted us to notice everything, especially the things nobody else was noticing.

Human interaction is always mysterious. The world of

pastoral care is equally so. Everybody has an agenda. Everybody wants to be in control. Everybody wants to appear healthy, good, competent, faithful, wise and caring. This applies as much to the caregiver as to the cared for. As we jockey for position, it's startlingly easy to make room for everybody and everything but God. Sometimes, however, God makes God's own way.

This visit was my all-time easiest job of temperature taking. It was like walking into a meat locker. Remember, this isn't about room temperature. It's about emotional temperature.

Some years ago our miniature schnauzer Friedrick (an exemplary companion of 14 years) became so weak that he could no longer stand. All the way to the veterinarian's office we dreaded and suspected what lay ahead. The first thing our veterinarian did upon examination was take Friedrick's temperature. He informed us, gently and sympathetically, that our pet's body temperature was already a couple of degrees below normal. He was dying. There really is a temperature to death.

Passing through the hospital corridor and taking its emotional temperature did nothing to prepare me for what I discovered as I crossed the threshold of this particular room. The patient was obviously clinically alive, but death was omnipresent. The emotional temperature was below freezing.

It was mid-afternoon in February and looked like snow. The sky was dark gray and forbidding and I was already worrying about my commute home. That day could have been the poster photo for the word "bleak," and the expansive window of the hospital room allowed it all in. An analyst of Bruegel's popular painting *Hunters in the Snow* once described it as *a distillation of pure cold.* (Timothy Foote, ed. *The World of Bruegel*, Time-Life Books, New York, 1968, p. 182.) This would have been an apt description of the view out that hospital window, and the room within.

The patient, a female in her late sixties, occupied the bed by the window. The other bed, the one nearest the door, was empty. Her chart indicated that she had been in the hospital four days, and yet there were no cards, flowers, magazines or other signs of support or caring in the room. Excluding necessary hospital equipment, the room was barren. She lay on her back staring out the window, covers pulled up to her chin. The lights in the room were off, apparently at the patient's request. The only illumination was the wan light from the window, somehow slipping through the thick, dark clouds outside.

I immediately experienced strong feelings of discomfort, bordering on fear and claustrophobia. I felt I had left the warm world behind and entered some dread alien land where breathing was out of style. I wanted to flee.

I'm still not sure why I didn't, so strong was my desire to bolt. Perhaps it was my Scotch-Irish stubbornness. Maybe it was something else. Who's to say why we stand and fight one time, and flee another?

Hello. I'm with the Chaplain's office. How are you today?

No flinch. No word. Nothing.

Is it all right if I visit with you for a minute?

Nothing. I stood there for a minute or more fighting the urge to flee from that awful spot.

Think it's going to snow?

Nothing. I stood there for another minute. *If I stay it will get better*, I told myself. It didn't.

I'm with the Chaplain's Office. I'm a Methodist minister working with the Chaplain's Office here. Would you like to talk? I was becoming pathetic and ridiculous, but I couldn't leave. My brain kept telling my feet to get going but they wouldn't move. And now my brain wouldn't listen either. I was becoming obnoxious and overly persistent. I was on the verge of blathering. I reminded myself of my mother who always told the checker at the supermarket, the bus driver, the clerk in the department store, the teller at the bank, whoever was at hand, whatever was on her mind at any given moment, embarrassing me no end.

The unrelenting "cold" in the room was becoming increasingly oppressive. Precipitation had finally begun outside, but it wasn't snow. It was sleeting, ticking hard now against the window. The wind was getting up.

I kept standing there and kept blathering, but I don't remember any more of what I said. Finally she had enough and interrupted me.

I'm going home tomorrow.

I pounced. Not only had I gotten a response, it was a positive response. She was going home!

So you're going home. You must be feeling better.

No. I'm dying. There's nothing more they can do for me. I'm going home to die.

The emotional temperature dropped several more degrees.

She had thrown down the gauntlet. If I was from the Chaplain's office and I wanted to talk, this was the moment. What did I have to say to that?

Do you have family to help you?

No. My husband died six years ago. We never had children. I have a sister who lives in Nebraska, but we aren't close. I guess the cab driver will help me to the door with my things.

Do you have neighbors who can help out?

I don't even know them.

Do you have a church family that can help?

I don't go to church.

The emotional temperature in the room was now lethal. I felt like I was dying too, just imagining what it was like to be her. I was imagining what her home looked like, felt like; cold, barren and emptily awaiting her return. I had stayed too long. I had been sucked into the world of that stark room. It no longer seemed to matter whether I stayed or left. I had nothing to offer, being powerless myself against the forces arrayed against her.

I wasn't even going to pray with her. I was going to apologize for intruding and go. I was staring dumbly and feeling as despairing and hopeless as I ever have when she spoke again.

Did you say you were Methodist?

I was startled. *Yes.*

I've always liked the Methodists. My Daddy liked them too. He said it was the Methodists that took us through the depression.

Really? How's that?

There was oxygen and some warmth in the room.

We lived on a farm in upstate New York. We had a huge vineyard. Even when it was hard to keep the rest of the farm going, the grapes always sold at a good price. We sold everything to the Welch's people and my Daddy said the Methodists kept Welch's in business. They needed their communion juice. She chuckled.

[88]

Honest to God, that woman chuckled.

Yes, Mam. I said, smiling. *We sure do need our communion juice.* Boy do we need our communion juice.

We didn't have any bread or juice, that woman and I. We only had each other, and the shared experience of what had been in that room when I entered, and what was in that room from the moment she started talking about those grapes.

And then she smiled. She really did. It wasn't a big, broad, goofy smile like the one I smiled when I responded to her about the juice, but it was a smile nevertheless.

Growing up on that farm must have been special. I said.

It was wonderful, she replied.

And then she told me of those happy days, describing the fields, barns, animals, family and her life there. As she did so, we both started to breathe more easily. She talked a lot about her father and what a character he was.

My experience of that moment was not one of pastoral care making a difference. It was not an experience of something taking the place of nothing, or of a void being filled. It was an experience of something chilling and quite terrible being driven out by something warm and good. A fledgling minister was clumsily handling a pastoral visit with a depressed hospital patient. It felt, however, as if the Archangel Michael were wielding his terrible swift sword and banishing demons back to hell.

When she finished talking, I asked her how she felt. She hesitated, and then smiled and said she felt *OK.* I prayed with her. She thanked me for coming and I finally left.

This time I felt that the world I reentered was the foreign soil. I felt like a time traveler. I drove the familiar commute home in something of a daze. The lousy driving conditions didn't bother me as they otherwise might have. It felt good to be ensconced in my cozy little VW beetle, with the heat on high, the wipers rhythmically keeping the sleet at bay, and visions of row upon row of plump concord grapes ripening under a summer sun.

The Angel?

As far as I know, I've never seen a ghost, leprechaun, gnome, troll, fairy, elf, river spirit, wood or mountain nymph, goblin, sprite, zombie, or snotgurgle (I got this one from a book about gnomes.) [Gnomes text by Wil Huygen, illustrated by Rien Povrtvliet, Harry N. Abrams, Inc. New York, 1977] Unlike Harry Potter, I've never seen a boggart, patronus, or blast-ended-skrewt. I may, however, have met and spoken with an angel. All I can do is tell the story.

My years as an Associate Minister were rife with struggle. Almost immediately, I began to understand the impossible limitations and expectations of the assignment, (or as a colleague once put it, my "tour of duty"), but the experience cut much deeper. I learned things about myself, about others, and especially about the church, that I didn't want to learn.

I learned that no matter how many times the Associate Minister visits, it's the Senior Minister folks want. (After just a couple of visits from me, most folks wanted to know if the Senior Minister was sick or on sabbatical.) Regardless of the effectiveness the Associate Minister's pastoral care (I always thought it inordinately effective), it was the Senior Minister's care most folks wanted.

I was expected to attend most committee meetings, but mine was never the definitive word. A lay person once succinctly characterized my sphere of influence during a committee meeting by quietly hearing me out, and then informing the rest of those present that, *He is a minister in training. I think it's time for us to hear from the fully-trained minister on staff, our Senior Minister.*

If the Associate Minister's preaching is as good as, or better than the Senior Pastor's, she or he will likely feel somewhat threatened and the Associate Minister will pay somewhere along the line. The Associate Minister will always be caught in the interminable power struggle between the Senior Minister and the rest of the staff. She or he will always be embroiled in some minor conflict or other and will always lose, and subsequently lose face with someone.

The Associate Minister will be introduced as *one of the pastor's at our church, our ASSISTANT minister, our junior pastor,* or *our student pastor.* Even if all of these things are quite true, they don't feel like much of an introduction.

Anger in the Associate Minister is read as jealousy. Career concern on the part of the Associate Minister is read as the worst sort of ambition. Unhappiness on the part of the Associate Minister is read as disloyalty that will inevitably lead to mutiny. Reserve is read as sullenness, joy as prideful bravado and success as overstepping one's bounds.

After eighteen months of this unparalleled joy, I was confused, unhappy, and doubting myself and my ministry. That's when I learned that I had narrowly missed an extraordinary career opportunity that my Bishop wanted for me. As they slowly unfolded, the sordid details of this missed opportunity found me doubting the veracity of colleagues, the church, God, my call, my present and my future. I felt hopeless, bitter and confused. I was slipping into depression.

In this midst of this slide, I arrived at the church early on a Wednesday morning seeking peace before the daily round of phone calls, meetings and general activity. Walking toward the office door from the church parking lot, I noticed a young, African-American male standing on the curb.

I was so accustomed to people seeking help from the church, and so absorbed in myself, that I didn't pay much attention to this man at the time. In retrospect, however, I realize that I noticed a host of incongruities right from the start. He wore a sport coat, slacks and shirt, all well worn and wrinkled, but also quite clean and comfortable looking. His shoes were dark and also much worn, but nevertheless appeared to fit well and looked comfortable. The clothes made an outfit that worked somehow. Earth tones.

His hair was cut short and a cloth bundle, which I assumed contained the rest of his earthly possessions, was slung across one shoulder. (It has always seemed so cliché that he carried his things in a cloth bundle, like the stereotypical hobo. All he lacked was the stick through the cloth knot.)

It was a lovely morning in early fall and the sexton and his assistant were sweeping the walkways just feet from where he stood. It was a startlingly beautiful tableau: the sun glistening brightly on the peaked roofs of the church buildings and nearby homes, the brick sidewalks bisecting patches of lawn still lushly green, fluttering birds, huge old oaks. A brick archway connecting the education/office building to the sanctuary framed the entire scene. He stood beneath the archway, by the office doors. Once again, it is only in retrospect that I realize I hadn't noticed until that moment what a glorious morning it was.

I had learned to be wary of the men who appeared at the church seeking handouts. I suspected their mental health and their capacity for violence. There had been incidents.

But I didn't feel fear that morning, perhaps due to his demeanor, or the others so close by, or my preoccupation with myself. I was annoyed that he was there.

I had come early for peace and stillness, not to process another transient looking for charity. The steady stream of these difficult, hard-living people had taken a toll of its own until I had become rather jaded. I no longer looked for Christ in their faces.

I remember looking into his face briefly, a healthy, serene, pleasant looking face. And he smelled good, or rather had no particular smell at all except that of clean. If clean has a smell, he exuded it. Most of those who came for help smelled very badly indeed. Their clothes were filthy with the oil of humanity, or reeked of alcohol, or tobacco, or kerosene, or wood smoke or all of the above. This transient was serene and clean.

I probably said *Good morning* by way of greeting him, but I don't remember. I know he said he wanted to talk with me. *Yeah,* I thought, *I'll bet you do. Come on in,* I said. He followed me as I unlocked doors and punched in the code to disable the alarm and in a few moments we were in my study. He sat in a chair across the desk from me as I dropped into my own chair, grabbed one of the in-house forms we used to process the church's relief fund and turned toward my typewriter. I asked him, rather dismissively I think, what he needed. I could as well have been a Department of Social Services worker three months from retirement.

In a soft, sure voice, he explained that he needed a bus ticket to someplace in the Midwest to attend the funeral of a relative. *Great*, I thought, *an easy one. He'll be out of here in no time.*

Did he know the way to the bus station? He sure did. I called to get the price of his ticket and departure time and reached my favorite bus-station clerk, the one most familiar with our procedures. The bus in question was leaving within the hour.

I explained this good fortune to the man, who simply smiled at me in reply. I swiveled around in my chair and began typing the required form. As I typed, I absently asked information of him for the form and he answered readily and to the point. Then came the lower part of the form where I filled in my explanation of his situation. As I typed, I could feel him staring at me. I could also feel his presence. It was so incredibly peaceful and, well, clean. I felt his eyes on me. I became self-conscious and uncomfortable.

And then he said the strangest thing. He said, *Do you know how fortunate you are to be so young and to have so much power?*

I was taken aback. I assumed he was referring to my power to decide whether or not he got a bus ticket, or whether another would get a hot meal, or a night in a motel, or an electric bill paid. I stopped typing, turned and looked at him. I said something in reply, but don't remember what.

He just kept smiling and staring at me, all serene and clean. I didn't feel threatened, but I felt very exposed.

I was ready for my guest to leave. I buzzed the secretaries' office and was relieved to discover that one of them had arrived. I explained that I was sending someone around the corner needing a voucher for the bus station.

I stood and handed over the form. He thanked me, still smiling, and left. I was glad he was gone. I was tired of feeling observed and exposed.

That's the story, except the secretary buzzed me that afternoon wondering when the man needing the bus ticket was ever going to come get his voucher. She wanted it off of her desk. I got that uncomfortable feeling again. Clean, serene and exposed.

I told her he needed to get to a funeral, and that his bus had left that morning. I described him. *No,* she said, no such person had ever walked around the corner.

I went looking for the sexton. *No,* he said, there had been no black man waiting on the sidewalk beneath the archway that morning. (He never missed a trick, our sexton, especially not the trick of a strange man standing by the church office door.)

I went looking for the sexton's assistant. Same story.

I went back to my study and phoned the bus station, asking for the same attendant. Nope. Nobody ever came. And he had been looked for.

I hung up the phone and looked over at that chair remembering what he had said. His question hadn't been about bus tickets, or motel rooms, or hot meals. *Do you know how fortunate you are to be so young and to have so much power?*

I didn't. Do we ever? His question haunts me yet as I wonder at its meanings.

Lilly

*W**armth. Light. Sweet darkness. Fast and slow my music, big and small sounds. Other thing sounds. Mama and Papa. Sweet sounds, warmth and light and music.*

Lilly was severely handicapped. There are medical names for the combination of deformities and handicaps she had but they are ultimately meaningless. She could not move, speak, or lift her head. She could hear and feel, and to some degree she could see.

Lilly's parents, Martha and William, discovered early that Lilly loved music. She communicated to them (a mystic communion beyond the words of earth to describe or comprehend) that her favorite music was country music. The radio on the dresser in her immaculate bedroom remained tuned to a country music station that never went off the air.

Mama and Papa. Just Mama. Just Papa. Soft and warm. Good steady sounds full of light. Then different. Not soft. Not deep.

Lilly was Martha and William's only child and was to them the most beautiful, special person God ever made.

The stress of care giving and their own aging and requisite physical problems sometimes forced one or the other to carry the burden of care alone for a time. Except it was never a burden. It was their joy. When I visited one or the other in the hospital during necessary stays there, each sought healing with intense determination. They were needed at home. They missed one another. They missed Lilly. They missed being together as a family.

Others. Not Mama. Not Papa. Not warmth and light. Not my world. Fumble touches.

Lilly was forty-three when the warm, deep light of her world here was superceded by the warm, deep light of heaven. For all of those years she was cared for by her parents and her cousin (a faithful and gifted physician), and visited by a few close family members and the succession of clergy sent to serve William, Martha and Lilly's home church. I was her minister for five years.

More other. More fumble. Silly ugly sounds.

Visiting Lilly was what I imagine visiting God to be, perhaps explaining my discomfort most of the time I was with her. I was unaccustomed to such profound grace; poorly conditioned for holy terrain.

Probably like all the ministers who visited Lilly, I mostly resorted to the making of sounds in her presence. Rather than simply partake of the holy peace and silence of her world, I read scripture and always left her with a prayer. Both must have sounded so foreign to her with their unnatural cadences and heft of emphasis. The Bibles themselves must have looked and sounded so strange. We came to her as ourselves, but soon diverted to our ordinations and our words.

Lilly could not comprehend our words, but she surely comprehended us. I'm convinced she knew more about me than I knew about her. I feared she knew more about me than I knew about myself.

Being with Lilly was threatening; unbearably honest and real. Even though she, the radio and I were the only ones in her room during my visits, it felt as if hosts of invisible others were there speaking a language beyond comprehension but well known to Lilly. It was at once electric and profoundly peaceful.

And so her ministers read scripture. We read for ourselves, and for protection from the unbearable brightness of Lilly's small bedroom. The intensity of that space overwhelmed us, so we cast the only spells we knew and watched them fall ineffectually about us, like rocks tossed at a hurricane.

Too intimidated to remain in Lilly's presence long enough to be healed, I yet sensed the depth and warmth and light of her world, but could neither hold nor bear it. It was, like Dickinson's hummingbird, *a route of evanescence* always beyond my grasp. Leaving her bedroom, I re-entered the world of shrillness, insufficient warmth, and dark places where the light of Lilly's world has not yet shone.

I reach to them. Reach with bright and warm. My world. Mama. Papa. Warm. Soft. Good.

ISBN 1-41205726-4